Walk by Faith
to Live Joyfully

by

Charles DeFeo

Published by:

BlueNose Press, Inc.
Printed in the United States of America
Published November, 2016

Nihil Obstat
Censor Librorum
Rev. Msgr. J. Brian Bransfield, S.T.D.

Imprimatur
Most Rev. Charles J. Chaput, O.F.M. Cap.
Archbishop of Philadelphia
November 3, 2016

The *Nihil Obstat* and *Imprimatur* are official declarations that a book or pamphlet is free of doctrinal or moral error. No implication is contained therein that those who have granted the *Nihil Obstat* and *Imprimatur* agree with the contents, opinions or statements expressed.

ISBN: 0997672013
ISBN-13: 9780997672015

For more information on this book
please visit: www.bluenosepress.com or
email the author at chasdefeo@yahoo.com

Book Cover design symbolizes The Light, Jesus, in a dark world, hence black and yellow, black is darkness, yellow is Sun or Son in this case. Walking by Faith to Live provides Joy and Light in your Life. We need to be the Light, reflect the Light in everything we do and say.

DEDICATION

This book is dedicated to Family, Life and Love; first, my Almighty and Triune Godhead, Father, who created me, Son, who redeemed me and Holy Spirit, who sanctifies me every day!

Second, my DeFeo family, past, present and future.

Third, my brothers and sisters in my faith family.

Life, Love and my Family are gifts from God, our Father and Creator and I appreciate all three and very grateful and thankful, never taking any for granted.

ENDORSEMENTS

Here's a book that will help you slow down before you end up where you don't want to go. It is written by a man who himself had to stop and decide where his life was going...I am grateful to God for the graces he gave to me and the wisdom he imparted through my own spiritual journey to help in some small way another companion headed in the same direction.

Rev. H. James Hutchins
Pastor Emeritus, St. Pius X Parish

Charles DeFeo has taken lemons and made lemonade. His honest, sincere approach to coming to terms with himself is moving and his words are useful to anyone who seeks help and understanding in our journey back to the Creator.

Stephen McWilliams, MFA, PhD
Author and Filmmaker, Villanova University

Charles DeFeo is no stranger to adversity, but he has learned an important lesson. No matter what happens to you in life, a personal relationship with Jesus Christ and the grace given through His Catholic Church will see you through. I admire Chas not only for his desire to keep going despite numerous personal struggles, but for his love of Jesus and desire to share him with others!

Gary Zimak
Catholic Speaker, Author and Radio Host
(www.followingthetruth.com)

Charles DeFeo has lots of beautiful things to say about healing a broken heart but it can all be summed up in five most important words: Keep your eyes on Christ.

Rose Sweet
Catholic Author and Speaker
Catholic's Divorce Survival Guide
(www.catholicsdivorce.com)

Charles DeFeo has written a concise, uplifting, and energizing spiritual "check-up" guide for the Year of Mercy. We know him as a spiritual brother, participant in the Catholic's Divorce Survival Guide ministry at St. Pius X, and, now, author. Chas has tapped into our Creator's survival guide. Read and re-read these gems of Truth. As he says, the key is to keep moving forward and never give up.

Mary Lou & Paul Brandt Butler
Facilitators
The Catholic's Divorce Survival Guide

Chas, I read your entire book as soon as I got it. I admire you very much and I am humbled by your passion and thirst for the Lord. I found it so easy to read. I never said a prayer for someone in an email before but here goes - Dear Lord on this snowy night I feel your love and warmth. Your precious son Chas radiates your love - may you watch over him and his family. Guide and comfort him in his walk through life. Thank you for his presence in my life. Amen. Stay warm Chasman and God bless!

Bernard Long
St. Pius X Men's Faith and Gospel Reflection Group
Parish Leader in Adult Faith Formation
"Brother" at City Team Ministries Volunteers Group

When many have left their faith or never quite found a personal relationship with The Lord; Charles gives a step by step account of his own personal journey to the Lord. He encourages all to enter into a relationship with the Greatest friend we will ever have... Jesus.

Kathleen McCarthy
Catholic Author, Speaker and Radio Host
In His Sign Network

"Chas DeFeo has given us in his book, a pithy and powerfully uplifting meditation on the healing journey of life. "Walk by Faith to Live Joyfully is short and easy to digest, yet filled with practical wisdom for any faith journey."

Mark Houck
President of The Kings Men;
Catholic Author, Speaker and Radio Host

INTRODUCTION

I wrote this book over the course of 2015 after attending an overnight retreat on December 31, 2014 whereby I consecrated 2015 to the Lord and asked Him to show me what He wants me to do for Him. I listened and heard in my inner sanctum "share your faith and love for me", so I started writing to glorify Him and help others in our common walk of faith.

Over the course of many years I always had the goal to write a book but had no idea what to write about.

In March of 2015 I suffered a mild heart attack and had a stent inserted in an artery within my heart so that changed my perspective.

This book is about my story, my family, how to overcome difficulties in life by clinging to and growing in faith in God under all circumstances, regardless of the good or bad and contains a collection of poems written by myself and 5 other family members. The majority of the poems were written by my Uncle Alex who also happened to be my godfather. His writings inspired my writings. He along with my parents, grandparents and brother was an important influence in my life. He loved his family and was always nearby.

It is incredibly important for men to be role models to the young. I have been blessed with great male role models. My father, brother and uncle modeled the faith to me and were great examples of authentic Christian masculinity. My mother is also a great role model as were my grandparents and other family members.

Let's get started on this journey together. Be prepared to open your mind and heart and learn something new about faith. Part of this book is a guide book to follow to help you pick yourself up and get out of difficult circumstances.

I hope and pray it helps you on your daily walk to start living a Joyful and Abundant life as I have learned to do through prayer, study and accepting the help and love of others.

May God bless you abundantly and may you start walking by faith to live joyfully even when you cannot see.

TABLE OF CONTENTS

FOREWARD

Years ago British agnostic Thomas Huxley had to leave early one morning to go from one speaking assignment to another. He got into a horse-drawn taxi and assumed that the hotel doorman had told the driver they were going to the train station. When he got in, he simply said to the driver, "Drive fast."

Off they went. After a short while, Huxley realized they were going in the opposite direction. He yelled to the driver, "Do you know where you're going?" Without looking back, the driver replied, "No, sir, but I'm driving very fast."

Many live their lives like that. Their schedule is overbooked and they are hustling from one place to another but without much thought to where they are going.

Here's a book that will help you slow down before you end up where you don't want to go. It is written by a man who himself had to stop and decide where his life was going. It took him a while to put on the brakes. He was going in the wrong direction but he turned to God and to all the help that God gave us travelers through the Church. He persevered. It took him a while before he was ready to go where God was leading. But he never abandoned God even as he searched for the right path. He kept seeking directions for his journey from people he assessed had the directions. With God's help he retraced his steps back to the road he had first set out on following God. And he hasn't been the same since.

As you read this book he has written recalling the directions God was giving him step by step, you will find a road map for yourself. Once you start reading, however, this man, once he got on the right road, drives very fast. It's a short book but it is filled, sentence after sentence, with the wisdom he gained on his journey. Don't try to go as fast as him. You'll miss the nuggets of wisdom contained in each sentence. Think about each sentence. Each sentence contains in it important steps in his journey. Think about each one. You will find a stepping stone in every sentence that will take you on an exciting journey to the heart of God.

I am grateful to God for the graces he gave to me and the wisdom he imparted through my own spiritual journey to help in some small way another companion headed in the same direction.

Rev. H. James Hutchins
Pastor Emeritus, St. Pius X Parish

Part I

Me and My Family

Faith, Family and Football

Chapter 1
I Want to Be the Man God Created Me to Be
My Story of Transformation

This is my story, what is yours? We all have a story, is God in your story?

I am a sales man by trade, and so blessed to be. It's a great way to make a living and I work for a company for many years now that treats me like family. I get to meet so many people, and work independently, and that's a blessing.

I am a football player at heart, and was blessed to be able to play for so many years and then coach for several years. To be able to be part of a band of brothers working so hard together, sweating and bleeding for a common cause provided no greater feeling in my deepest core.

Playing sports while growing up as a young boy, and having the opportunity to play football through high school and college helped shape and mold me into the man I have become. This was only second to the influence of my parents, my brother, my extended family members and training and instruction in the Catholic faith. As a lifelong practicing Catholic, my way has been set, even though both good and evil have run parallel courses in my life starting at age 9 on Good Friday.

Football teaches obedience, discipline and teamwork. These are all qualities we all need to grow in holiness and become the body of Jesus Christ, who is my Lord, Savior, King and everything!

Being Catholic is like being a football player; obedience, discipline and teamwork are needed to succeed. I am part of a team, the community of saints. My playbook now is my bible. My weekly game plan is the Catechism of The Catholic Church. I need to study both to become the best player I can be; the best version of myself and the man God has called me to become.

These two books work together in forming my conscience or catechizing me properly as we say in the Catholic Church. They also work together to give me backbone, help me stand strong in the Faith, and resist the devil and temptation.

Stand for Something or
You Will Fall for Anything

I say this to my children often so I need to live it. I don't want to be a do as I say person, I want to be a do as I do person, because everything I do, God willing, is following in the footsteps of Jesus!

I am a sinner, a member of the human race, fallen due to Original Sin. I do not despair; however, I have hope and joy! Because God, Our Father, sent us Jesus, who came to save us from our sins!

I Live, Love and Laugh!!!

I cherish each day and moment spent with family and friends. I am thankful for my job and for my profession which I have worked in for over 30 years and it has been an incredible blessing in my life.

I have an attitude of gratitude, and my altitude is determined by my attitude. I am thankful to all those along my life's journey who have loved, helped and supported me in any way.

Jesus gave us the Beatitudes and I encourage you to memorize and pray them every day as I have and do!

I was transformed starting on March 18, 2015, the day I admitted myself to the hospital due to chest pain.

I received three sacraments while in the hospital, Confession and Communion, which I choose to receive on regular basis, always have and always will.

I was incredibly blessed to receive Anointing of the Sick by my friend, Fr. Ugo. This was the first time I received the sacrament of Anointing of the Sick. A sacrament is a sensible sign, instituted by Jesus, to provide God's grace or His life within us, and it is supernatural.

The Anointing of the sick healed me and cleansed me in every way from concupiscence, like I have never experienced before. I encourage you to receive it if you are gravely ill, near death or elderly and extremely frail. You don't have to be near death to receive it. Go and ask your priest if he will administer it to you or research the Church's canon law on who can administer and who can receive this sacrament; only a priest or bishop can administer. Since we are all fallen and sinful by nature it can and will heal you both physically and spiritually if you are sick enough to be able to receive it. This does not mean you nor I will never sin again or be tempted, but it helps us. It also does not mean you or I will be miraculously cured of an illness. We must always cooperate with God's grace and freely choose to receive the sacrament worthily and in humility and contrition and unite our suffering with Christ's and offer it up for others and accept God's will regardless of the outcome. Never waste suffering! Make it redemptive as Jesus showed us.

I received this sacrament on the evening of March 19, 2015, also the feast of St. Joseph, who is the foster father of Jesus and who I am devoted to and ask his intercession to be a better man and father every day!

The next day, March 20, I had my procedure where a stent was inserted into the circumflex artery of my heart to help clear plaque that had built up and was stopping blood flow to my heart.

The procedure did not go smoothly and had to be completed twice. This time period was the middle of Lent. I was in the process of my Lenten sacrifices and experienced great peace and mercy from my Lord and Savior Jesus Christ while I was in the hospital these four days.

Sue and the kids were great and there for me, as well as friends. The prayers and thoughts were very important to my outcome.

I was alone, but not alone! Jesus was always with me! I never let go of my rosary. The hospital staff ended up taping it to my left hand during the procedure.

I was blessed to experience and meditate on the Passion and wounds of Christ, which I experienced in miniature in and on my body as both of my wrists had to be pierced at separate times due to the first procedure not going smoothly. In addition, most of my upper torso was marked up and bruised from the monitors that had to be placed on and stuck in and on me and the intravenous and needles that had to be inserted.

11

I lay in a cold white room on a skinny table during the procedure. The doctors and nurses were great.

I had to hold both of my arms higher than my heart for hours because of the arteries that were pierced in my wrists to help with blood flow. It is very unusual for the procedure not to go smoothly and to have to be repeated, and opening up the arteries in both wrists. This was not what everyone wanted to do, but was necessary because I suffered a mild heart attack during the first procedure. This caused the procedure to be repeated, however my wrist was clamped so blood would not flow out; therefore, they had to open my other wrist.

After the second procedure, I laid on my back for hours with arms raised skyward. It was uncomfortable to say the least but allowed me to realize the pain, agony and discomfort Jesus must have experienced on His cross. This was my cross, and I was uniting my little cross to the massive Cross of Christ and offering this up for sinners and the dying.

Transformation started that day, and continues daily with the help of prayer from the supernatural Angelic Warfare Confraternity as well as my "brothers" and "sisters" in faith and the support and love of my family and friends.

We journey together, even if not always on the same page, and not headed in same direction all the time. I am incredibly blessed, so much so, it is overwhelming and difficult to put into words.

God will never be outdone in generosity if only we let Him in, even just a little bit! He is the greatest running back of all times! Reason being, just like a great running in football needs a little crack or space from his offensive line and blockers to burst through the line of scrimmage on his way to the end zone, God gives us free will to choose Him or reject Him. He never forces us to follow Him. So, if we give Him a little crack or opening in our hearts, He will do the rest!

Hence, I have been transformed by His Love and Mercy, changed forever for the Good, and walking daily toward Him. Won't you allow His Holy Spirit to transform you as well? It is a process, take baby steps. Keep growing, learning, praying and studying our faith and go deeper every day!

Always cultivate a positive outlook and attitude, even in the face of persecution, rejection and evil. Accept the things you cannot change, change the things you can, pray for the wisdom to know the difference!

I started this chapter by stating I tell my children often to stand for something or fall for anything.

I stand for Jesus first and foremost, His body, blood and word, and the teachings of The Catholic Church through its Catechism.

How about you? What do you stand for? What will you stand for?

I am called to serve, called to witness, called to preach the Gospel of my Lord and Savior Jesus Christ; the Gospel of true Love, Peace and Mercy! The Truth!!!

Chapter 2
God Made Us a Family

A Bible verse that speaks to me regarding Jesus' view of family is from Luke 8:21 – "He said to them in reply, 'My Mother and my brothers are those who hear the word of God and act on it.'"

Another Bible verse geared toward raising children speaks to me as well – "train a boy in the way he should go; / even when he is old, he will not swerve from it" – Proverbs 22:6. I think my dad said that! He drilled so much wisdom in my head it was a little dizzying at times, but I am so thankful and grateful for it. I always heeded his advice and it was always good advice.

Difficult to accept sometimes, but nevertheless, our families are not always on the same page when it comes to faith. My friend Fr. Ugo says this before our Kairos retreats with the high school boys and girls. It's important to meet people where they are at in the present.

I believe in brutal honesty. My father, God rest his soul, drilled that philosophy of honesty into me at a very young age. Lying was absolutely the single most thing that drove him over the edge. So with that said, I have written this chapter about my family with honesty. This chapter is geared specifically toward my children as I have written separate

15

chapters on my family of origin, my mother, father and brother.

God has blessed me with four wonderful children and a nephew, who I became legal guardian of, too. My marital situation is disorderly in the words of The Catechism of the Catholic Church, which I am devoted to and follow the teachings of 100%. I don't dismiss that, but keep moving forward in faith, flaws included. The woman I married on November 24, 1990 goes by Sue. I would like to explain a little about Sue and my children:

SUE – stands for Sharpening. She may be the single most person in the world who God uses to test me. Even though we are estranged, we built something together and she is the mother of my children, a good person and a good mother.

ALEX – means strong man. He is a worker with a strong will, always has been, with a quiet strength and confidence. I like to call him Aggie, got that from my younger girls as when they very young they could not pronounce Alex.

JULIA – means youthful. She shares similar traits that I have in me. I like to call her joyous, she does make me laugh with her cunning ways.

ANGELA – means Angel or Angelic. I call her Amazing. She has a number of natural gifts and she can be really intense.

ROSALIE – we call her Ross or Rosie! A Rose is the most beautiful flower in my opinion. When Rosie was really young she kept us all in stitches without even trying. I think Rosie is actually very mature beyond her age.

My Brother Kenny's children are very important to me as well. I will start with Guy, Kenny's youngest, because he came to live with us halfway through High School, and I became his legal guardian. As I write in a separate chapter, his father was my older brother, and only sibling. He passed when Guy was nine.

Guy's full name is Robert Guy DeFeo. He goes by Guy. Both of his grandfathers were named Robert. Guy stands for Gregarious to say the least. He was voted most flirtatious in High School after only attending the high school for two years. He really does have a loving heart, even though he prefers to talk rather than listen.

Rebecca is Kenny's oldest. She is very humble and caring.

Last, but certainly not least, is Jennifer, who has a flair and smile that can captivate.

Kenny's children all have children and families of their own now.

I don't believe I am too hard on my children, but I do expect and demand more from them because that is the way I was raised. I can be compassionate and understanding to acquaintances and strangers, but not so to my own children sometimes.

Some people use the term disconnected. That is the way I feel toward my own children at times, and probably what they feel toward me. However, I am always there for them, and their biggest fan, even if I don't listen to them or understand them all the time.

I expect them to share my faith in God and practice it the way I do, but that can be unrealistic. I pray for them every day and love being in their presence. I love when we are all together, and I also love being with them individually.

One of my favorite things to do with each of them is take them out for a special dinner when they have a birthday. I call it the Birthday dinner. I got this idea from my brother Kenny, many years ago. They really seem to embrace it and enjoy it, and it means a lot to me. I think I get more out of it than they do. It is a great event to look forward to. What I like most is when we put the cell phones down and just talk. I always feel like I listen my best to them at this moment, not preaching, not telling them what I think they should do or be, just listening and the conversation seems to go very well. I really need to work on doing that with them more often.

I enjoy doing anything with my girls, like shopping or just hanging out. I love going to watch them play sports or other activities. Angela sings and has a beautiful voice and takes great pictures, for example.

Alex, Guy and I love sports, especially football. I know I definitely raised Alex the right way because he is a diehard Eagles fan, just like me, and that warms my heart. I have held Eagles Seasons tickets for over 20 seasons now, and my most enjoyable moments are going to the games with Alex and Guy. We have shared many memorable moments at these games.

I like to say Faith, Family, and Football! And I really do try to live that. Wholesome recreational activity is needed to refresh our spirits, and a couple of hours of a diversion as long as it's not sinful can renew us.

Even Jesus showed us this by retreating from the crowds to be alone in prayer with His Father, but also to be with others at parties. He never appeared to turn down an invitation.

Honestly, I do wish all of my children shared my passion for my faith and my father's faith (my mother's faith too). They say the family goes where the father goes when it comes to faith, somehow I broke the mold. But, I have faith in God, and trust Him, even though I doubt sometimes, and you never know what is really in a person's heart. I believe the Holy Spirit works and acts in everyone's life even if a person does not recognize or acknowledge God. It's an inside job, and often God's timetable is not the same as ours. Even if it never happens, I am thankful to be blessed with my children who teach me how to be a better father, often.

Children are amazing and life changing. They make you open up, they make you want to sacrifice for them, and they truly are an image of God's love in good times and bad. They symbolize two people becoming one in the flesh and love of God. Witnessing the birth of your child is miraculous. It is overwhelming and brings tears to your eyes. A newborn baby is pure joy, then you watch them grow into a toddler, a young person, a teenager, and then an adult.

Yes, there are ups and downs, happy and sad moments, and they get hurt sometimes, physically, emotionally and mentally. However, there are great moments of victory and joy as well, and as a parent you are always there for them. Something else my father would say, "Just be there, show up every day"!

I just hope and pray I can impart my wisdom and faith on my children like my father did to me. All we can do as parents is love, with the love Jesus taught us called Agape (sacrificial love, putting the good of the other above your own good).

We are still works in progress, and I am excited to see my children's lives unfold before my very eyes and to be there with them for it.

As I mentioned earlier Guy, Rebecca and Jennifer have beautiful children of their own and great families too. Rebecca and Jenn live far away, so I don't get to see them much, but I enjoy texting them often. Thank God for technology.

Guy lives close, and has a daughter named Layla. Rebecca, Jennifer and Guy are now raising the next generation. Layla has brought even more joy to our family and Guy's wife Melanie is yet another "daughter" for me to enjoy, love and laugh with as well as learn from.

I don't know what the future brings, it's in God's hands, but I am glad I am going to face it with the people God has placed in my life that I call family.

I would like to close with one of my favorite poems from *Favorite Catholic Prayers* called "God Made Us a Family":

21

We Need One Another,
We Love One Another,
We Forgive One Another,
We Work Together,
We Play Together,
We Worship Together,
Together We Use God's Word,
Together We Grow in Christ,
Together We Love All Men,
Together We Serve Our God,
Together We Hope for Heaven,
These Are Our Hopes and Ideals,
Help Us to Attain Them O God,
Through Jesus Christ Our Lord,
In and Through the Power of the Holy Spirit!

As we learned from the World Meeting of Families held in Philadelphia, let us celebrate our families and all families. Pray for each other to strengthen families as that was the purpose of this event, and know that God and Our Church is not a God and Church that excludes, but includes.

I love my DeFeo family, past, present and future.

I love my "brothers" and "sisters" in the faith and I love my fellow brothers and sisters who are citizens in this world with me.

I believe we are all God's children no matter who you are, what you believe or where you come from.

I love all my relatives; DeFeo's, Gentile's, Pacetti's and Cavarocchi's, and my in-laws, friends, acquaintances, and even strangers I have met over the years.

Every person we meet has a purpose in our lives and touches us in different ways.

I hope and pray we treat each other worldwide as God would want us to.

God bless!

Chapter 3
My Father
I called him Pop

My Pop was born Robert Charles DeFeo on July 7, 1938. He passed from this life into the next on June 21, 2008. He left a lasting legacy and impression on me that lives in me forever.

He, along with my mother and God, gave me life. He nurtured, protected, provided for and led me and his family in many ways. I am forever grateful for his presence in my life and thankful to God for him. He shaped me to become the man I am today. He was a real man, not just because he was tough, although he was, but because he sacrificed and gave of himself. He shared and passed on his faith with and to me.

For as long as I can remember, he brought my brother and me to church every Sunday. We never missed Sunday Mass. He made sure we went, and he always went with us. We would get there on time, and not leave before the Mass ended. He would take us to The Sacrament of Confession at least a couple of times a year when we were young. He would go to Confession, and not just make sure we went, but he would go as well. He would take us out for dinner afterwards and we would talk.

When I went away to college, we would talk by phone every Sunday. There were no cell phones at this time, only land lines, so no texting either. He would always ask if I went to church. I never wanted to lie to him so I usually went. He is the number one reason I never fell away from the church. I did miss Sunday Mass occasionally, but I never stayed away for any kind of long period. I have never let an entire year go by in my lifetime without attending Confession. I go regularly to confession now, once a month and have gone weekly if I feel it was necessary. It's our faith, let's live it! I live it because of my father. He still influences me even though I no longer have his physical presence in my life.

My father and mother would lead the tailgate parties after my football games when I played in college. Many of their friends would come to my games not because of me, but because of my parents. They would always have the biggest group of tailgaters around them. My pop loved that.

He also ran many trips to college football games including Penn State and Notre Dame. He was an excitable guy and fun to be around. He liked excitement, sports and competition. It really energized him. Boy, could he energize others.

He was a coach as well, a football coach mostly. It still warms my heart today when I run into his former players, or just anyone who knew him. They tell me a story about him, how much he meant to them, how he taught them the game, or more importantly what he taught them about life. Many people say kind words about him, and how he touched their lives in a positive way.

He had passion for God and compassion for man. He had passion for life, period. He loved my mother with passion and zeal and he loved life with passion and zeal. He had ups and downs throughout life, like most have. His life was struck with much tragedy, losing his sister, niece (god-child) and both parents within a period of 7 years, all while he was only in his 20's.

Later on he would lose his son and my older brother, his brother, and his mother-in-law and father-in-law. He was the last member of his original family before he passed.

Through it all he acted with dignity, grace, courage and a strength I have rarely witnessed. Not only did his faith in God and practice of his Catholic faith and heritage never waver, it got stronger. He loved Jesus! He loved talking about Jesus' love for us, and he would often say "The Cross before me, The World behind me" and "Jesus in me loves you"!

My father was a great speaker, even though he never finished college. He went to Temple for one year and played football there. He left school after a year and

27

went out into the working world. He was blue-collar, hard worker, but very street smart and wise. He would drill words to live by in my head. Some of his favorite things to say were: "It's nice to be important, but more important to be nice". "Take care of your money when you are young, and it will take care of you when you are old". "The building is put up for education, not for sports" (it was so important to him for my brother and I to complete our college degrees even though he did not). "What does it profit a man to gain the whole world, but forfeit his soul". "It's easier for a camel to pass through the eye of a needle than for a rich man to enter heaven". "The cross before me, the world behind me". He recited many other sayings too. Many of these quotes are biblical and come from Jesus.

Our family name, DeFeo, was very important to him. He wanted my brother and I to respect who we were, where we came from, and the importance of our family heritage. I know we both always did.

He was always writing notes to himself so he would not forget anything, yet his mind was like a computer. He could remember numbers, phone numbers, and stats off the top of his head like no one else I knew.

He hated to tell jokes and he hated to be told jokes, yet no one could make me laugh as hard as he.

I loved being around him, but especially as I became an adult. In adulthood, he became my best friend. He liked to walk for miles, and I walked with him often for many years. We would talk. He needed to vent and blow off steam when we walked, and I let him.

When he and my mom moved away to Florida, every time I would call or go visit him and my mom, or when they would come back to visit with and stay with me, he was always so excited to see me and hear my voice and he would always scream out "CHASAROO" excitedly with so much love. We would always hug and kiss each other, and he always told me he loved me and he was proud of me. I would say I love you and I am proud of you too, Pop. I still am proud of him, and he lives on in me.

He loved being a Grandpop and Great Grandpop. I know because I heard him proudly tell others often.

Below is a poem written by my uncle and god-father, and my Pop's brother, Alex. I think it best captures the kind of man my father was. The poem was written about a little local tap-room bar where my father was the day manager.

"The OUTPOST"
It's three miles from 69th street, but a hundred miles
     away
It's a family bar with men, who meet there every day.

Joe O'Donnell is the owner, a man who's fair and kind
And the Manager is Bob DeFeo, the best you'll ever find.
It's a sports bar featuring football, mainly O'Hara and Bonner High.
These O'Donnell men are loyal, and will be until they die.
The fans of these two high schools, meet each Friday night at seven
And to drink and root at the outpost is a ticket up to Heaven!
(Written by my uncle, Alexander J. DeFeo, October 12, 1987)

I love you Pop and miss you, but still feel you very near. I know you told me to be strong when you had to leave me, and I am heeding your advice to show up and be there every day!

Thanks for being you!

Love,
Your son, Charles "Chasaroo" DeFeo

Chapter 4
A Mother's Love
My Mother's Love for Me

...a mom along with God's and a father's help, gives you the gift of life and brings you into this world.

...a mom nurtures you when you are a baby, feeds you, changes you, cleans you, teaches you and plays with you. She does most everything for you and sacrifices most everything for you.

...a mom lies on her back when you are a baby and toddler, and puts you on her feet and moves them up and down until you laugh, and she laughs along with you.

...a mom holds you when you are scared because it's raining fiercely and thunder and lightning too. She tucks you in, reads, talks or tells stories until you are comforted.

...a mom believes in you even when you are not sure you believe in yourself.

...a mom has a catch with you, helps you hit a ball, or does whatever it takes to help you be better at the sport you are playing.

...a mom helps you become a better student, helps you with your homework, projects (I will never forget the grade school project we did together when we used my Action Jackson figure as Moses, and the Styrofoam board as floor and wall and drew the burning bush - God - on it.) I loved that project and doing it with you.

...a mom drops you off at your first day of High School when you are really nervous and assures you it will be OK, because thousands have gone before you and done it. She says you are more special than the rest anyway. She makes your lunch every day and drives you to school and you talk.

...a mom provides by example a work ethic that is unmatched. She does this not just by telling, but by rolling her sleeves up and doing, not just when she was young but her entire life and even now in her late 70's! Cleaning like a professional, cooking, caring, sharing, working, winning awards at work because of hard work, and having a great attitude and all the while smiling.

...a mom gives her son pep talks, and even tough love while in high school and college playing football.

...a mom shares and practices her faith with you, and passes down her family and faith legacy, not just in words but in actions.

...a mom watches her son, husband, and both parents pass from this life to the next with dignity, grace and faith while she is left behind.

...a mom is a leader who inspires confidence in her adult son to believe he can and will succeed.

...a mom is not perfect, and makes mistakes in her life and in her marriage, but loves her husband and two sons with a passion and determination that is unmatched.

...a mom becomes your best friend, ally, confidant, and mentor. She is everything even though you don't always return the same love she gives to you all the time.

...a mom stands by you in good times and bad, ups and downs, never judging, always helping, never taking, always giving.

...a mom brings home the bacon, can support herself and her family, fry it up in a pan and never let her husband forget he is a man.

...there are so many other things a mom can do. I don't know about a mom, or another mom, I can only speak of my mom, and she is all of the above and more. Her name is Elodia (Pacetti) DeFeo and she goes by Dee or Dee Dee as my father affectionately called her, and she was born 10/10/1939.

Mom, I love you. Thank you for loving me so much, for being you, and letting me be me. I will always value and treasure everything you have given me in this life. From the way I look, to family values, to faith in God, to devotion to Our Blessed Mother, to respecting myself and others, to a strong work ethic and perseverance, to being a little mischievous too, and realizing it's OK to have a little fun.

You are the best! Always will be! I used to love the way Pop always said how beautiful you are, and how he wanted to build a monument to you. I also loved when Kenny visited you and greeted you with the biggest bear hug.

We still are a great family, because of your love! God Bless You Forever and a day!

Happy Mother's Day!

With Much Love,
Your son Charles DeFeo
May 7, 2012

(This is an original poem I wrote to and for my mother as her Mother's day present in 2012.)

Chapter 5
Kenny – My Brother
"I can do all things through
He who strengthens me"

Kenny was my brother. My one and only sibling, he was four and half years older than I, and had a huge impact on my life in every way. Next to my father, Kenny was the most influential man in my life. He was born February 25, 1960 and named Kenneth Charles DeFeo. My father was a good teacher in many ways, and Kenny was the ultimate pupil. He had so much going for him, handsome, smart, athletic, kind and humble.

We played together when we were young. Our family was a package deal, since I was younger I was always there at every sporting event he ever played. I was kind of the mascot for many of the teams he played on. As we grew older, we became more than brothers. We were great friends. He was my mentor, guardian and meant everything to me. I was his sidekick.

My brother was well liked by everyone: adults, girls, boys, and animals. I never heard anyone say anything bad about him.

He was a star in just about everything throughout grade school, high school, college and life. I never ever heard him talk about himself or his accomplishments. He would always find something nice to say about someone else. He would always pump them up instead of himself.

One of his high school friends told me he would leave money under his plate when he came over and had a meal. He was such a gentleman. Several women that went to school with him still beam about him when they speak of him.

A woman who went to grade school with Kenny actually had tears in her eyes when she spoke of how nice and kind he was toward her.

I am not joking when I write that Kenny was a living saint to me and others. Sister Agnes, who taught Kenny in high school while at Monsignor Bonner said it best – "Kenny DeFeo had goodness written all over his face". Kenny was an honor student, member of student council, National Honor society, natural born leader, very good athlete and tremendous football player".

For all of his goodness and kindness, I can honestly say when he played sports he was an absolute terror. Maybe the toughest I have ever seen on any level. In High School, he was elected captain of the football and baseball teams. He helped lead the varsity baseball team to the league championship game as a junior. He threw the shotput for the track team. He was actually a good basketball player as well, however football is the sport where he made his mark. Before he graduated high school, he had won every award imaginable. I can tell you he would have traded all the individual awards in for a team championship. He was selected all-league twice, all-county and honorable mention All-State. He was touted in pre-season before his senior football season as an All-American. This was in spite of playing on a losing team and with a nagging injury. He never missed a play. He was an interior lineman so there was no glory for him. He was awarded the John Cappelletti award at Bonner, given to the student who most exemplifies Bonner High inside and outside the classroom and on the fields of play. Teachers loved him. I run into teachers today who still speak very highly of him.

Kenny was such an amazing football player, even at a young age. When he was playing little league football for my father who was the coach of his team then, (yes, he had a great teacher, have I mentioned that?) he started at center when he was eleven years old on a team and in a league that had players as old as fourteen!

Back to high school, Kenny started in football at Bonner as a sophomore, junior and senior on both Offense and Defense. He hardly ever got a break, and he was rarely taken out for three straight seasons. That is a rare accomplishment! I went to and played for a different high school. Our coach would not even let anyone, no matter how good you were, start on both offense and defense in the same game.

Kenny and my friend Gerry Feehrey, who played at arch rival Cardinal O'Hara, where I went, were the two best lineman in the league and county. They were in the same grade and were rivals throughout grade school and High School. O'Hara was a much stronger team, one of the best in the area.

Gerry was one of the toughest to play the game, after High School he went to Syracuse where he starred and captained the team. As an undrafted free agent rookie in 1983, Gerry earned a spot on the Eagles and eventually became the starting center. He had close to a ten year NFL career. I am blessed to call Gerry friend, and to have gotten to coach with him during the 2014 season at O'Hara high school.

Gerry and Kenny developed a friendship and respect for each other out of rivalry. The reason I bring this up is during those days, games in high school playing against each other, Kenny had to go nose to nose with Gerry while on defense and then turn around and play offense having to block against an O'Hara Linebacker who also went on to play Division 1 college football. Again, O'Hara players were not allowed to play on both offense and defense. Those guys got to rest and take a break while Kenny never came off the field except for a few special team plays. All of this while nursing an injury no one even knew about. O'Hara won the game by a wide margin and Kenny gave all the credit to those guys. Believe me, he played tough and had a good game.

Gerry and Kenny always gave equal praise to each other, and I will never forget Gerry's kind gesture after Kenny's passing. Gerry called the newspaper and made sure they wrote a nice article and obituary.

After high school graduation, Kenny attended the United States Naval Academy and had a very good freshman season on the freshman team. At that time, freshman could only play on the freshman team. He became an expert marksman with a gun at the Naval Academy as well as being graded as a top boxer and wrestler, all things required at the Academy. Things didn't work out for him, and he quickly transferred out and attended Community College for a semester and then enrolling at Villanova University. He was a walk on to the Villanova football team in 1979. He was ineligible to play that season due to transfer status, and thus not awarded a scholarship.

My brother had such a quiet strength and determination. It was really scary. During the 1979 season, Kenny could only practice with the team. He was relegated to scout team, and my parents paid for his college. Kenny was never one to feel sorry for himself, or wait for something to happen. He made things happen. Instead of sulking on the scout team, and that word was not even in his vocabulary, he played every practice like his life depended on it. The team was pretty good that year, and had some great players. Howie Long, who went on and starred in the NFL, and became an NFL hall of famer was on that team. Two other players, one of which went on to finish his college career as starter for Ohio State, after Villanova dropped its football program after the 1980 season, went on to start at linebacker for The Cleveland Browns, and the other was a defensive back who went on to start in the USFL. They had many other good players on the Villanova defense as well. Kenny played offense so he had to block these guys during practice.

Kenny did a great job, and he was overwhelmingly great to the point that these players who were stars were not too happy with him because they protected themselves and did not want to get hurt. After two weeks of playing on the scout team, the coaches decided to award him a full scholarship and put him on the roster. I would like to add that the great Howie Long, did not enjoy having to face Kenny. I am not proposing that Howie was scared, but Howie knew that this was practice and that he would have to exert maximum effort in practice when facing Kenny. Kenny played with such a high motor all the time it was frightening, and even though he was always the shortest lineman, only 5'11", he was so powerfully built at 250 lbs., He was incredibly strong, quick off the ball and fearless! He was really hard for anyone to handle.

How did I know all this? I had inside information.

When I played football at Ursinus College, one of Villanova's coaches at the time Kenny was there coached me at Ursinus. In addition, one of Kenny's teammates and good friend while at Villanova also became a coach at Ursinus. These two men told me these stories.

In the 1980 season, Kenny earned a starting position on the offensive line and helped the team to a winning record. The Villanova administration decided to drop the football program even though they were a good team, citing financial reasons.

My brother had two years of college eligibility left and wanted to continue to play so he had to transfer yet again. He showed great perseverance and a positive attitude. He went to, what is now called, The University of Memphis. Within 3 months he became the team's starting center, was named Team Captain, and awarded MVP of the team (as an offensive lineman!) This was unheard of! The team was not very successful, but Kenny finished a great individual career while at Memphis. He got to play in the New Orleans Superdome against Tulane. He also got to play nose to nose in games against two all-time greats, Reggie White and Bruce Smith.

Additionally, he played against a Herschel Walker led Georgia Bulldog team who was ranked number 1 in the country at the time, and against the Bobby Bowden led Florida State Seminoles. All of Memphis' home games were played in the beautiful Liberty Bowl stadium. Kenny was given press by Memphis as a pre-season Outland trophy candidate before the 1981 season. The Outland trophy is awarded to the "best" offensive lineman in college football. As I said earlier, the team was not successful, and it's hard to achieve individual awards when your team does not win games very often. Kenny was named All-Metro Conference center.

Kenny never complained. He worked so hard I can't even tell you. He, along with my father and mother, is the reason I had a successful high school and small college football career. The season before my junior year in high school, while Kenny was still playing at Villanova, he took me under his wing for weightlifting, training, running, agility, and nutrition. He showed me what it takes to become a real football player. I probably held him back because I was younger, smaller and not as strong. He could have been training with his college teammates, but that was the kind of person he was. I owe a lot to Kenny, and through all this adversity Kenny faced his faith grew stronger.

Kenny's college football career and ultimately his entire football career ended at Memphis. He went undrafted by both the USFL and NFL. The Seattle Seahawks worked him out, but his lack of height caused all of the teams to refrain from drafting him. His college coach wanted to help him get a rookie free agent tryout with a team, but ultimately he decided not to try out. He was reluctant to move yet again, and he was planning to be married. He loved Memphis, so he graduated and went into the trucking industry as a manager.

Memphis is in the heart of the Baptist bible belt. Kenny got involved with the Fellowship of Christian Athletes while playing football at Memphis, and became a practicing Baptist. Remember, he was born and raised Catholic like me. This was really hard for my parents to understand, and they did not like it. I was only eighteen at the time so I was not sure what to make of this. However, Kenny was the most-sincere person I knew. He put his heart and soul into everything he did, just like our Pop taught us to do. He absolutely believed he was doing the right thing, and he came to know and love Jesus like no person I had ever known. In less than a year, it appeared he had the Bible memorized. He was so loving and compassionate and never condemned anyone, but he lived the faith that he now practiced. He gave me a bible and a prayer book and I read them cover to cover. My parents ultimately grew in faith because God used Kenny as His instrument.

Growing up the four of us, my parents Kenny and I, were a tight knit group. As time marches on, my dad liked to say, "As the children become adults, things change especially if you move far away, but that's life and God's plan sometimes. Kenny has 3 beautiful children, all adults, with families of their own, and I am proud of them. Kenny worked in the trucking industry in management, all of his life. He became a faithful and practicing Baptist until he passed on from this life suddenly from a heart attack at age 37, on December 28, 1997.

God works in mysterious ways. He used Kenny to increase the faith life in our family. We actually became more Catholic, and grew deeper in our faith. We studied and read scripture and the teachings of The Catholic Church.

When I visited my brother, we would go to his church, and when he returned home, he would go to ours.

We stayed as close as possible for living so far away from each other. We spoke by phone about every week, and we would never say goodbye without saying I love you and I am proud of you to each other. He would always say it first. He was my biggest fan, and I was his biggest fan.

I miss him and it would have been nice to grow old together and talk and share life. However, God had other plans. He, like my Pop, are both now angel's on my shoulders.

Kenny's high school friends started a memorial scholarship in his name in 1998, and the scholarship still maintains to this day.

Kenny DeFeo was inducted into his High School Hall of fame posthumously in 2006. He was also inducted into the Pennsylvania Sports Hall of Fame, Delaware County Chapter in 2009.

I still run into people today, and when I tell them my name they ask if I am related to Kenny DeFeo. When they realize that we were brothers, they often tell me that he was a legend.

I am honored when people call me Kenny as they sometimes do. I am honored to be his brother and have known him for thirty-three years. My parents handled his death with grace, dignity and strong faith in God. They always said that Kenny was a gift to them for 37 years. Kenny was a gift to many and touched the lives of many people all over the country. He has 5 grandchildren, and I will make sure they all remember the kind of man he was. He was good and kind, yet one of the toughest there ever was. He was most importantly a child of God, follower of Jesus and inspiration to many.

I love you Kenny DeFeo, and I am proud of you! Rest in Peace in the loving arms of your beloved Jesus forever! You make me proud to be the brand DeFeo! Thank you for strengthening me and sharpening me. Even though you are physically gone from us, I will make sure you are never forgotten. We are brothers forever!

Chapter 6
Who are my brothers,
sisters and family?

Since this book is about faith, family and football, I would be remiss if I did not mention my brothers and sisters in the Catholic Faith. As I stated earlier in this book, my parents, brother, and other family members, like my Uncle Alex, were people who practiced our faith and passed it down to me. We stand on the shoulders of our parents, grandparents and other family members in every way including our faith. I am thankful to them for passing the faith on to me, as well as the love, affection, support and belief in me.

As Jesus stated when he was talking to a group, and someone approached Him saying your mother and other family members were outside, Jesus replied in the Gospel of Matthew 12:48, "Who are my mother and my brothers? Those who do the will of God". Jesus was not trying to be difficult, he was extending His family to believers, not just "blood" relations.

I am blessed to have many friends and mentors in the faith, but most importantly my brothers in our weekly St. Pius X men's faith sharing group. I also

47

have my brothers and sisters in my monthly Dominican Lay group who are truly family in the faith in addition to my "blood" relatives. They sharpen and strengthen me in love, and help me to grow in the love and knowledge of God, just as my "blood" relations do.

I encourage you to find and commit to meeting with a group of faith brothers and/or sisters. If you do this, community will be like nothing you ever experienced before and will help you, with God's grace, become the best version of yourself.

You can set the world on fire!

May God Bless you and keep you walking!

Part II

How Do We Live

A Joy Filled Life?

Chapter 7
Happiness and Joy

Matthew 6:33 – "But seek first the kingdom [of God] and his righteousness, and all these things will be given you besides."

What is happiness? How do we find joy, peace, power and passion in our vocation as; married, single, divorced, widowed, while still being Catholic?

If you are not Catholic, this book will help you regardless of your faith. However, you must read it with an open heart and mind.

A good way to start is to fall in Love with your faith; I did.

We will focus on Peace and Happiness in this chapter.

What makes you happy? Write a mission statement as to what really makes you happy. If material wealth, other people, or things make you happy, start thinking outside of yourself. Are you happier by giving something or getting something? Change your thought process.

Start by praying. Everything begins with prayer. Happiness begins with prayer. Pray for others. Start by praying for your loved ones. Say a prayer of Thanksgiving for all God has done for you in good times and bad. You have the gift of life, love, friendship, health, housing, food, money, and transportation. Pray for life, our Pope, peace on earth, our politicians, and the souls in purgatory. Pray for our families, friends, our enemies, or those who dislike us. How could anyone dislike us? That would be impossible, right?

Have fun with being you. Have fun being alone. Have fun in the presence of God! Are you aware that when you are alone, you are in the presence of God? When you are with others you are in the presence of God. We sometimes just think we are only in the presence of God when we are in Church, at Mass, in Eucharistic adoration or praying.

Think about the times you are most happy. Are you glorifying God when you are most happy? Regardless of where you are, or who you are with, are you with God? When you are at your child's game, recital, with a friend, at mass or praying or maybe even out for a walk or jog, are you with God? If you are not, try bringing God in. Just say thank you Jesus first, then say it out loud, and then pray it out loud. Take baby steps. You and I are a work in progress regardless of what stage of faith we are at. Try it! Practice an attitude of gratitude all the time, no matter where you are, who you are with or what you are doing. Try it even when you are alone, and watch your happiness grow! As Matthew 6:33 tells us, "But seek first the kingdom [of God] and his righteousness, and all these things will be given you besides."

Chapter 8
Are you in denial or shock due to divorce, death of spouse, or any other tribulation?

"We know that all things work for good for those who love God, who are called according to his purpose." – Romans 8:28

This is one of my favorite scripture quotes and I rely on it daily.

Whenever tragedy strikes this is a great quote to lean on. Let us never forget that our Lord and Savior Jesus Christ, has turned everything upside down and has made all things new. What appears to be tragedy to you, may be a blessing from God. One of my favorite songs is called "Blessings" by Laura Story. The theme of the song is, what if our teardrops were God's blessings in disguise?

I have personally been through shock and denial. I lost my only sibling, my older brother, to death in 1997. He was only 37 years old. He was my brother, friend, mentor, and confidant. He meant a lot to me, and he taught me much about life and faith. I lost my father to death in 2008. My father and I had a great and loving relationship. My father instilled his values and his Catholic faith into me. I would not be the man I am today without my father's and brother's influence. They are the two most influential men in my life.

As much as I loved my father and brother, the separation of my marriage in 2008 was the most devastating event of my life. Worse than death! When I realized my wife and I were not going to make it, I felt like dying. My first reaction was shock and denial, "how can this happen to me"? I cried like a baby. I was not even angry because I was so shocked. I had a difficult time functioning. I could not think, read or focus on anything.

I, of course, blamed my wife for everything, because it was her choice not mine. I wanted to do anything to help and repair our marriage. How could she choose this? How could she do this? This was not really happening? This was a bad dream!

I was numb for years! As my wife moved on with her life, I felt abandoned and left behind. We had 4 children together that we loved.

Not only did I blame God, but I cursed God! I had no idea at that time that God had a plan for my life.

Romans 8:28 tells us what to do. He tells us what to focus on, and that is to keep loving Him. If we love Him, we will be called according to His purpose.

I wasn't there yet. Although I did not stop loving God, I certainly did not turn to Him for love, security and acceptance. That was a big mistake. Denial holds us back from facing the truth because we cannot accept it. When we continue to deny the truth, we are not able to accept or focus on reality and we cannot move forward. I do not like to use the term "move on", but the term, "keep moving forward" is necessary for not just survival but to thrive. God wants us to thrive! His plans are grandiose for our lives in this world and the next!

We are all told there are many stages when tragedy strikes. The first stage is shock and denial. The next two stages are worse, but as you navigate through shock and denial try to focus on God's love and loving Him.

A good prayer to say repeatedly, while in this first stage is – "I love you Jesus, thank you Jesus, help me Jesus." You may be wondering why you would say thank you Jesus, but we can never forget what He did for us. I also strongly believe we should thank Him for the good and bad in our lives. Every little thing that happens to us, is an opportunity for us to grow closer to Him. We are on a journey to heaven, and I hope and pray we all live a long happy life. However, we must remember, our final destination is heaven. Our lives on this earth are a gift from God. God wants us to enjoy this life with family and friends. Go and live the abundant life that God wants us to live.

In addition to leaning on God, lean on good friends who genuinely care. Try not to whine to them. I have certainly done my share of whining, it will take place, but know you will grow out of it and this too shall pass.

I strongly recommend meeting with a small group of faith based friends regularly, even weekly. If you are a man, find a group of faith based men. If you are a woman, find other women. It is very important to seek out others of the same sex, when you are in the denial stage. They must have a strong faith and practice and study their Catholicism. If your parish does not have a group, check to see if a neighboring parish has a group. Consider starting one at your own parish. I started my own group with my friend. Stick with this group. You will soon find out many in the group have their own set of problems, but all share the faith. My men's faith sharing and Gospel Reflection group at St. Pius X parish is in Broomall, PA. They are very important to me, and we now meet socially after years of meeting together weekly. We started the group in May, 2008. My father passed about five weeks later, and the first people that knocked on my door was this group of friends. When you are in a crisis, there is no greater friendship then the friendship of those you share the faith with. God, our faith and our friends in the faith, are a rock and refuge like no other!

I would also recommend attending Eucharistic Adoration. There is no greater comfort than sitting in front of our Lord in the Holy Sacrament. Start with baby steps if you must, 5-10 minutes, but the goal is to work up to an hour a week, every week. Devote yourself to that weekly hour with Jesus exposed in the Blessed Sacrament. As one saint said to another saint when he was asked what to do during Eucharistic Adoration, the saint replied, "Nothing, I look at Him and He looks at me and we are happy together" (this is attributed to St. John Vianney). That is an awesome thought! Pray if you wish, say the rosary or read a holy book, but try to do nothing and just let God speak to you. As the prophet Samuel said, "Speak, for your servant is listening" (1 Samuel 3:10).

Serve others. Go to a shelter or soup kitchen or help children in need, but actively participate. Do this all in the name of Jesus. Serving brings a smile to our faces and warms our hearts. It takes the emphasis off of ourselves when we think and help others. It distracts our pain and misery. It makes us count our blessings and all that is good in our lives.

Find a constructive hobby. Do anything you like, as long as it is constructive. I play in a bocce ball league. I love it and have fun. I am a long time Eagles football season ticket holder and take my son and nephew to most games. I love spending time with them, and we enjoy football together. A couple hours a week of wholesome distraction is good and needed. So if you like golf, cards, cooking or whatever, go and do it!

I am involved with other groups and activities as well and run a scholarship fund in my deceased brother's name. It is one of the most rewarding things I do.

I hope you found some of the advice in this chapter helpful. While you work through the denial stage, meditate on Romans 8:28. It has worked for me. Also, realize there will be ups and downs, and not all the stages are clear cut. You will go back and forth throughout the various stages. Whatever stage you are in, focus on God's love!

Chapter 9
Anger and Bitterness

Philippians 4:13 tells us "I have the strength for everything through him who empowers me."

The Him is Jesus Christ! When it comes to anger and bitterness we can use all the help we can get. Don't go it alone. Own it, admit it, and ask for God's help. Nail it to the cross! This is the first bible verse I memorized at age 18. My brother Kenny gave me a plaque for Christmas that year with this verse on it, and I still cherish it to this day.

We come out of shock and denial, and we are angry. Who are you angry with? A spouse? God? The other person? Everyone maybe? We are in a rage and angry at everyone. Maybe we are angry at no one except ourselves. Maybe we feel guilty as well. I will save guilt for the next chapter so let's focus on anger.

Is anger ever a good thing? Maybe it sometimes can be if we can use it for good. Go back to the Romans 8:28 reference. Even Jesus became angry. We know He was because scripture tells us He overthrew the money changers tables in the Temple. He made a chord to use as a whip to drive them out. Jesus said, "...It is written, 'My house shall be a house of prayer, but you have made it a den of thieves.'" (Luke 19:46). It also says, "Zeal for your house will consume me." (cf. Psalm 69:10; John 2:17)

So, zeal for my house or my marriage consumed me. How do you handle this anger? You may need to get professional help, and that is ok. If you are diagnosed with any kind of mental illness or depression, you may be advised to take medication. Follow doctor's orders. If you prefer to meet with a psychiatrist or psychologist who is faith based, then by all means do. If you have strong faith, it is not necessary or mandatory that you do.

I would however, strongly recommend finding a spiritual adviser to meet with regularly. It may be best not to meet with a priest friend or religious who you are too friendly with or who knows your spouse as well. Spiritual guidance may be best to come from a religious who is grounded and trained in the area of spiritual guidance. It may be best to find your closest retreat center and go to one of the clergy at the center who specifically are spiritual directors. Go on a retreat. There is nothing better than going on retreat. Turn off your phone and all electronic devices and be quiet and still for days! "Be still and confess that I am God!" (Psalm 46:11).

Retreats are very cleansing in so many ways. Retreats slow our minds down, take the focus off our anger, and enable us to connect with God's love. Anger is real and has to be managed. Proper diet and exercise is very important. It helps our bodies and minds function properly and reduces stress and anger.

Enjoy friends at this time. Find new friends too, and focus on the friendship and the activity at that time. Live in the moment! Try not to dwell on the past, or worry about the future. Don't worry about if you fit in, just enjoy the time spent together. Do not put burdensome expectations on yourself or the other person. Try meeting with friends in a group.

Anger is a very difficult stage. Anger will subside over time. Anger may rear its ugly head when you least expect it. When you feel anger, it may be best to leave or walk away from whoever or whatever is making you angry at the time and pray! Pray whatever prayer pops into your head, but it may be better to have a prayer plan, like the Rosary. Pray for the other person or party making you angry at the time. Focus on your breathing as well. Your breath is the breath of God in you and it is very calming.

It is ok to be angry and feel angry, just don't dwell on it or let it consume you. Do whatever you have to do to take your thoughts off the anger.

Memorizing favorite scripture passages and calling them to mind when angry also helps.

Reward yourself when you overcome or diffuse anger. It is a great victory over self. Positive thoughts, healthy thoughts, constructive thoughts and actions are always best for you.

CHAPTER 10
Guilt

Psalm 118:8 – "Better to take refuge in the LORD / than to put one's trust in mortals."

If you are divorced or in process of divorce, you most likely have felt some guilt. This may be especially true if you have children. "Why did this happen?", "What could I have done differently?", "Is this my fault?".

We all feel guilt from time to time. Be honest and open with your children, ask them to be honest and open with you. It is ok for you to get angry, and it is ok for your children to get angry. Open and honest communication is a must to overcome guilt. Don't let anything stew! Don't let your mind work on you negatively. Find an accountability partner, or a trusted friend, who shares your faith in God. When you are feeling depressed and or guilty talk to them about it. Don't just spend money on your children to overcome guilt. Give your time to your children. Quantity and quality time are important. It does not matter what you do with your children, just be with them. There is comfort for them and you just by being in same room with them. Play a game, read a book, share a story, watch a movie or TV. Eat a meal together. Take a walk or a ride together.

If you are unable to be with your kids every day because of divorce or separation, then call, text or email them. Ask them what they are doing. Share a favorite scripture quote or family line you say together. Tell them you love them. Be genuine, but be creative! Send a selfie picture to them or a picture of the two of you. Reach out to your children every day. Text them to say goodnight. If you miss a day reaching out to them, just do it the next day.

If your children play sports or other activities, go to see them play as much as possible. Pick them up or drop them off at home afterward. You are not just doing this for them, you are doing it for you. Do it because you want to!

Change your way of thinking and your behavior. Stop saying you are sorry. Provide lots of hugs, kisses, fist bumps and just genuinely care. One of my favorite things to do is bless all my children by signing their forehead before I leave them (making the sign of the cross on their forehead), and we say a Hail Mary together. They have come to expect it, never complain, or ask me to stop. I think they like when I do that. We also pray and say grace before every meal, even in public. We hold hands, stop and pray.

If you feel guilty often, it will take time to overcome. Try these steps and remember it takes time to change thoughts and behavior. It will even feel uncomfortable at first, but keep persevering. Stay positive! It takes about three weeks for something new to become a habit. We create good habits as well as bad habits. Persevere in creating good habits, and work hard to eliminate bad habits, thoughts and actions.

As Psalm 118:8 tells us, "Better to take refuge in the LORD / than to put one's trust in mortals."

Turn your guilt over to God, and trust Him to take care of it.

Chapter 11
Depression

Ephesians 5:20 – "Giving thanks always and for everything in the name of our Lord Jesus Christ to God the Father."

Depression is a serious medical illness; it is not something that you have made up in your head. This definition comes to us from www.nimh.nih.gov.

Depression may be described as feeling sad, blue, unhappy, miserable, or down in the dumps. Most of us feel this way at one time or another for short periods.

From the Mayo clinic – "Depression is a mood disorder that causes a persistent feeling of sadness and loss of interest". Also called major depression, major depressive disorder or clinical depression, it affects how you feel, think and behave and can lead to a variety of emotional and physical problems. You may have trouble doing normal day to day activities, and depression may make you feel as if life isn't worth living.

More than just a bout of the blues, depression isn't a weakness, nor is it something that you can simply 'snap out' of. Depression may require long term treatment. But don't get discouraged. Most people with depression feel better with medication, psychological counselling or both. Other treatments also may help."

I am not a doctor, psychologist, theologian or spiritual guide and can only talk from personal experience on depression. It is serious and if you have clinical depression, please go get professional help.

As I mentioned earlier, spiritual guidance is recommended but get professional help as well.

Does the above sound familiar? If you have experienced marital divorce or separation, chances are you have experienced symptoms of depression. If the symptoms of feeling down, unmotivated or lacking energy persist for weeks or months go seek professional help, in my opinion.

Another important thing to practice is don't isolate yourself for long periods. Isolation is necessary for all of us at times. Be it a spiritual retreat, or just spending time alone with yourself. You have to be comfortable with being alone and you need to do that. If you are continually isolating yourself, ask yourself why. This could be a problem as well.

That is why partaking in a small faith based group that meets regularly is so important. You will build friendships based on rock!

Is God's grace sufficient for you? Are you allowing God's strength to replace your weakness? The great Apostle St. Paul may have suffered depression. Read Acts of the Apostles, Romans and all his epistles to learn more. Try reading 1 Kings Chapter 19, which describes the anguish, depression and suicidal thoughts of the great prophet Elijah. A number of saints experienced and/or suffered from depression as well.

Try reading the lives of these saints and be blessed to gain more insight:

Blessed Father Enrico Rebuschini, Servants of God Cleonilde Guerra, Wiera Ida Francia, Fr. Bill Atkinson, St. Padre Pio, St. Theresa Liseux, St. Theresa of Calcutta, St. John Vianney, St. Benedict

Joseph Labre, St. Dymphna, St. John of The Cross, St. Theresa of Avila and St. Elizabeth Ann Seton.

These great saints always found peace in their great faith and prayer life. They also found peace in their holy companions. They did not let anything, including great suffering and/or mental illness or anguish keep them from the love of God and living lives of heroic virtue. You and I can do it too!

Don't go it alone. Nail it to the cross. Nail all your pain and suffering to the cross. Jesus wants us to. Lean on a community of believers you meet with regularly. Ask them to pray for you.

Ephesians 5:20 tells us, "Giving thanks always and for everything in the name of our Lord Jesus Christ to God the Father."

We are to give the good and the bad, the joy and the suffering over to God. We need to thank Him for all of it. Your depression could even be the springboard for you to achieve greatness. My depression resulted in the writing of this book.

Again, you know your own body best. If you think you have clinical depression, I cannot stress enough to you, to go get help. Anxiety, depression, bipolar disorder, all stem from the same tree and need to be treated professionally.

Always be prayerful in everything you do. Always give the glory to our Lord and Savior Jesus Christ, and seek out those professionals He gifted to help us!

I was diagnosed as bipolar 2, which is a milder form, but once diagnosed it is treatable and absolutely can be managed. You can live an abundant life and fully function in any manner.

Live a balanced life! Get 8 hours sleep! "Early to bed and early to rise". Eat healthy, and eat a lot of fruits and vegetables. Drink a lot of water. Exercise! Read positive and uplifting books and articles. Build relationships, especially with Jesus! Put God first, and everything else will be taken care.

Chapter 12
Healing and Holiness

Luke 1:46-47 – "…My soul proclaims the greatness of the Lord; / my spirit rejoices in God my savior."

1 Peter 1:16 - "Be holy because I [am] holy."

We can heal through holiness. Holiness is not a one-time thing. It is an all the time thing! This doesn't mean you will never stumble or sin. Why did Jesus give us the Sacrament of Confession? To help us when we stumble, fall and sin. Confession should not be a laundry list, but it is an encounter with God! It is God's grace within us! We are restored to right relationship with Him when we partake sincerely in the Sacrament of Reconciliation. The sacrament of Reconciliation is a tremendous gift to us from our Lord and Savior Jesus Christ!

We are called to sanctify our day, every day, at our waking hour. Roll out of bed, drop to your knees, and give thanks to the Lord for a peaceful night sleep. Thank Him for the gift of the day before us. Ask God to bless everything you will experience this day, and to be holy in every thought, word and deed you will perform. Ask Him to help you do everything you do to glorify his name.

We are works in progress. It is a lifelong process. In our faith, our holiness and our healing, there will be ups and downs.

Follow the lives of the saints, and they will lead you to healing, holiness and ultimately to Jesus! The saints are our friends on the journey; on the path to healing and holiness on the Way! Jesus is the Way. The saints cannot do anything but lead us to Jesus.

Healing and Holiness go hand in hand. Start with prayer. In addition to prayer, study is necessary. Take baby steps, but you cannot go it alone. You also cannot go with just Jesus and you, and no one else.

Jesus picked twelve Apostles and other disciples to share in His work. He wants us to be in relationship. If you have and build relationships with others, and they are sincere in their faith walk, it will help you heal and become Holy.

Practice the Sacraments. You cannot heal and become Holy without practicing the sacraments. Go to Mass and Communion every Sunday at least!

Confess your sins to a priest regularly. I would suggest once a month.

You have already been baptized and received Confirmation. You and I are called to be soldiers for Jesus Christ!

In addition to practicing your Catholic faith, join and partake in a small group of faith sharing friends, who meet once a week, and reflect on the Gospel.

Serve the poor regularly, or find a cause you enjoy. Look in your church bulletin, or go to your parish rectory and inquire about such activities.

A Pro-Life group is a wonderful and rewarding opportunity. If you like animals, serve in an animal shelter. If you have knowledge of a sport, coach a team of children or teenagers. Teach in your parish Religious education program. Whatever you are good at, go do it! Make sure you are serving others in the name of and for the glory of God!

By practicing your faith, living it, praying, studying, meeting with, worshipping with a community of believers, and serving in the name of God, will come healing and holiness. It all works together for the glory of God. Please God first, and you will grow in holiness, heal mentally, emotionally, and spiritually.

As our Blessed Mother proclaimed "My soul proclaims the greatness of the Lord; / my spirit rejoices in God my savior." This was her Magnificat. (Luke 1:46-47)

Our Lady also proclaimed, "Behold, I am the handmaid of the Lord. May it be done to me according to your word." Her Fiat! Her faith! (Luke 1:38)

Trust and Love the Lord "with all your heart, with all your soul, and with all your mind." (Matthew 22:37)

Chapter 13
Acceptance and Moving Forward

Exodus 3:14 – "I am who am."

We have experienced shock, denial, anger, bitterness, guilt, depression, healing and holiness; how do we accept our situation and move forward? It's not easy. It was not easy for me, I did not have seamless transitions where I moved through and out of each stage into the next. The stages overlap and we can backslide. I know I have, and continue to do so.

How do we finally accept our circumstances?

Maybe the best advice is given to us by Almighty God himself.

Exodus 3:14 – "I am who am".

This still does not make acceptance any easier. Unless you were in an abusive marriage and the only way not to be physically, emotionally or mentally injured was to leave. Acceptance and moving forward is very difficult.

81

Let me explain further, when one spouse has decided the marriage is over from "irreconcilable differences", but the other spouse has not really done anything deserving of the marriage to end, nor wants the marriage to end, it can be so difficult to accept. This can be especially hard if you have not had marriage counselling, and you are willing to go to marriage counselling.

Let me stop here and address any person or couple whose marriage still has a chance. Young couples who may be reading this who are happily married; never stop sharpening your "axe". What I mean by sharpening your axe, is work on your marriage continually. Spending time together and having date nights whether you have children or not is very important. More important, I encourage you to attend an annual marriage encounter retreat for a weekend together.

If for some reason you are not very religious, or not religious at all, and you are still reading this book, thank you! I advise you to go to an annual religious, or even non-religious marriage encounter weekend. If you are contemplating religion, even better, I hope your spouse is as well. Go talk with a priest or clergymen.

Back to acceptance for those who cannot accept their current separation or divorced circumstances. Lean on St. Paul, who preached and lived this. Under all circumstances, good and bad, he gave thanks to God and made the best of the situation.

I don't like to use the term "move on", I prefer moving forward. Even when we cannot understand where we are going and why, we need to keep moving forward. That means, keep working in your job. Keep exercising and eating right, and keep meeting with friends. First and foremost, spend lots of time with your children even if you don't live with them. Get creative, pick them up from school, sports and activities. Offer to drive them and friends places. Go shopping with them. Go for ice cream. Do whatever you like, or you both like.

Get involved with some activity or group you have been planning to join. Serve the community or less fortunate. "That will make you appreciate what you have, not what you don't". My Pop always used to say that.

Make new friends, and connect with old friends. Don't just go for having a relationship with a person of opposite sex. Stop focusing on your needs, wants, desires, and seek God's will for your life!

You may learn to accept your circumstances, or you may not, but you will keep moving forward. Learn better how to discern God's will for your life, and you will become "who you are". Never forget we are a work in progress until the day we die!

Chapter 14
Divorced or Separated

Acts 7:60 – "Lord, do not hold this sin against them."

Are you lonely? Me too! Join the club.

You may be surrounded by many family members and friends who care about you, but you still feel lonely. Why isn't our relationship with Jesus enough to fill our emptiness? It should be, right? I still ask myself that question. I also feel guilty for it not being enough.

Jesus, help me! Jesus, I love you! Jesus, thank you! Jesus, I believe, help my unbelief!

Regardless of how you feel, never stop loving your family members and friends who love you and care about you.

Find a spiritual advisor. Never stop growing deeper in your faith, and be honest with yourself. If you desire to have a partner of the opposite sex to have a "romantic" relationship with, maybe God has other plans for you. Talk to God about it, even if you are mad at Him, talk to Him about this.

I am not a proponent for online dating services, but I would recommend, if you are going to try that, to find the most reputable and faith based one. I have investigated some of these, and although I am not an expert in this field, I encourage you strongly not to rush into a relationship but to focus on friendship. Focus on the friends of both sexes you currently know and trust. I also feel strongly that you should not think about dating until you are divorced, and your marriage has been nullified by the Church. I am not an expert on Nullity of Marriage either, and recommend you at least learn the truth about it. Try reading Rose Sweet's book, "How to Understand and Petition for Your Decree of Nullity" (A Little Book with Big Help). It is part of the Catholic's Divorce Survival guide series.

Do not beat yourself up too much while reviewing why your marriage failed. I have done this and continue to as well. At first, I blamed my wife, 100 percent. I was a bit blindsided. I was aware we had problems in our relationship. She wanted to end the marriage, and I did not. I thought it was all her fault. I tried to offer to go to counseling, especially marriage encounters, and religious workshops that I thought would help and heal our broken relationship. She was not interested in that, but never offered an alternative. I was angry at her, God, and myself, but did not even know why I was angry at myself.

As time and years went by, I started to reflect on our failed marriage. I started to blame myself mostly. How could I let this happen? What did I do to harm our marriage? These questions were bad and also prideful, which was awful. I had to stop!

We have to go to Jesus, even if we are not feeling it. We also have to go to a man of the cloth, a priest, who is trained in spiritual guidance. If you need psychological help and medication because you seriously have a condition like depression or Bi-polar, then please get treated for it. I also strongly recommend meeting with a spiritual advisor who is trained in spiritual advising. It's ok to talk and share your psychological conditions and problems with your spiritual advisor, but the main focus is to grow in your Catholic Faith. If you practice a different faith, grow in it. If you do not practice any faith, I encourage you to go online and find the United States Conference of Catholic Bishops. Start reading or find and read information on the Catholic Church. It's so beautiful! I will let you decide why or why not.

I strongly recommend anyone who is divorced or in process of divorce to meet with a spiritual advisor. Also learn about the Annulment process from someone trained and read the book I mentioned above on the "Nullity of Divorce".

Never stop living and never stop moving forward in your business or profession. Move forward in your personal life, and understand that moving forward is not the same thing as moving on. Moving on is much more difficult, but never let your feelings get in the way of doing your job to the best of your ability. Never let your feelings allow you to isolate old friends who care about you. Make new friends along the way. Never ever let your feelings stop you from loving your children or spending quality and quantity time with them. Never demean your spouse to your children or anyone for that matter. Give your anger, frustration or struggle over to Jesus, who welcomes you. Whether you are right or wrong, He will make you see the light.

Focus on friendship! If you meet someone or like someone of opposite sex, and are attracted to them, when you are with them, focus on friendship. Don't look for, or expect anything more than that.

If you are separated but not yet divorced, first and foremost, always be open to reconciliation with your spouse. Never close the door on that, and remain faithful to your marriage vows. Matrimony is a Sacrament. God's plan from the beginning did not include divorce. This is another reason why you need a spiritual advisor. Make sure you take the spiritual advisor's advice because it's God advice. Take the advice whether you like it or not, and whether you agree with it or not.

Lastly, even though you are divorced or separated, you are not dead. Keep living, loving and laughing. Build relationships and serve others. Find out what you can do in your parish, and volunteer. Find things you like or have interest in and go do it.

In Acts 7:60, St. Stephen, our first martyr, as he was dying, shouted, "Lord, do not hold this sin against them."

Please don't hold a grudge against your spouse, it only hurts you and hold's you back from growing. No matter how difficult, pray for your ex-spouse. Pray especially for his or her conversion in heart, and for their heart to turn to God. Ask Him to help them seek his ways, because everything else will be added.

Pray for conversion in your heart every day as well.

We have to wake up every morning and consecrate our hearts, minds and souls to serve God every day. A good thing to partake in is the 33 days to morning glory program, as I did. It is a total consecration to the Sacred Heart of Jesus, through the immaculate heart of Mary. It has made all the difference for me. Never forget, you are alone, but not alone!

Chapter 15
Widowed or Never Married

Luke 21:1-4 (The Widow's Offering)

This Bible passage about the widow's mite, has more to do with detachment from material possession and putting complete trust in God in all things. I cannot speak to being a widow or widower. I can speak to what it means for all men, women regardless of being single or married to put our trust in God.

If you are widowed, first and foremost, my condolences. I am very sorry for your great loss. I have lost close loved ones, but those who were genuinely in love as husband and wife, after losing a spouse, I can only imagine what it must feel like when a part of you is gone.

I would suggest finding a small group of others who are widowed, who share common interests, and meet regularly. If it is a faith based group, even better.

Don't allow loneliness or bitterness to define who you are. Cherish the memories. Let them warm your heart on a cold winter night. Acknowledge and accept the good times and bad you shared. Thank God for the blessings, and the time you had together on this earth because it is all a gift.

Live, love and laugh with your children and grandchildren if you were blessed with both, and if not then live, love and laugh with your other family members and friends.

Never forget the special dates. Remember wedding anniversaries, birthdays, and even day of death and burial. Cry if you must. Visit the gravesite if you are inclined, and always bring God into it. Talk to Him as you would talk to a friend, because He wants to be your intimate friend.

Find a new hobby, or keep at an old one. I play in a bocce ball league. My team is called "Men of Faith", and it is made up of my friends from my parish men's faith group. I am also a longtime Philadelphia Eagles football season ticket holder, and I attend games with my son, nephew, daughters and friends. It's a great time to spend time with those I love.

Call an old friend. Make a new friend, and keep seeing your friends. Volunteer. There is nothing like giving back your time and talent to those who need, or would enjoy and appreciate it.

Don't let anyone, even a close family member, tell you what you should be doing. If you don't want to move, don't. If you do want to move, do it. Loved ones should just be there and listen, unless you ask for their advice.

Don't do anything drastic for at least one year after you have lost your spouse. Keep your routine the same. If it will change, let it happen gradually and naturally. If you want to be alone it is ok to ask for space. Always ask with a thankful attitude.

Make sure you are making the decisions with God's help. Do not let anyone else force you to do anything against your will.

Be sensible in all things, especially finances. See your financial planner, and have honest dialogue. Do the same with your tax preparer and anyone else involved with your finances.

Most of all keep moving forward. In my opinion it is ok NOT to move on if you don't want to, but keep moving forward and stay in touch with God. In your personal life continue to practice your faith and worship with a community of believers.

The same advice given above goes for all those single people who never married. If you have never married, seek out your parish's information on groups for singles' activities. The Knights of Columbus, a Catholic men's group, is a wonderful organization. It is a brotherhood to consider joining. You can live out your faith in this group.

If you experience same sex attraction, but want to live out your faith in a chaste manner, you can join and/or partake in all these same organizations and small groups of faith sharing as well. Look into a group called Courage International.

All men and women regardless of sexual persuasion who are single and want to commit to living a chaste life in every way are called by The Catholic Church to live out the unique talents God has bestowed on you. You can do this in an abundant and joyful life. I can tell you from personal experience, that I am experiencing more joy by living a chaste life than I have in almost twenty years.

I am attracted to adult women, however self-mastery over our sexual desires and controlling them instead of it controlling you or me is true freedom. This pertains to both hetero-sexual and homo-sexual people.

Chastity has to do with what we read, listen to, speak, how we dress, and our sexual behavior. Chastity is living in a manner becoming to God's will for our lives in total purity in body, mind and heart.

Chapter 16
How Do We Sharpen Each Other?

"As iron sharpens iron, / so man sharpens his fellow man." – Proverbs 27:17

This is one of my favorite Bible quotes and I learned it from my www.thekingsmen.org brothers. It is their official bible quote and used on all of their merchandise.

I believe we sharpen each other by living in The Word and sharing it. In this chapter I will share the teachings of the Church, and my favorite Bible quotes and prayers of The Church.

Let's get started.

Everything starts and comes forth from with The Liturgy of The Word and The Liturgy of The Eucharist (Jesus instituted the Liturgy of The Eucharist during The Last Supper Passover meal he shared with His Apostles on what we now call Holy Thursday, see John 14:1-16:33). We call it, The Mass, which takes place daily throughout the world.

Let's back up a little.

What does Catholic mean? It means Universal.

The Church is One, Holy, Catholic and Apostolic. This comes directly from Jesus: "so that they may all be one, as you, Father, are in me and I in you, that they also may be in us, that the world may believe that you sent me." – John 17:21.

The prayers of the church start with The Mass. (The Liturgy of the Word and The Liturgy of The Eucharist). Next, we have The Liturgy of Hours (these are prayers that include scripture passages and writings of our Church Fathers, Saints and Popes, hymns and psalms said and prayed at specific hours throughout the day, every day, hence, Liturgy of Hours) that priests and religious are required to pray daily. All of the faithful, including lay people are encouraged to pray these prayers as well.

The Holy Rosary is also to be prayed daily. It is a meditation on the life of Jesus through the eyes of His Blessed Mother. This prayer is a powerful weapon against evil, and is so much more than just repeating our Apostles Creed, Hail Mary's, Our Father's and Doxology (Glory Be prayer).

The rosary beads make a circle that start at the cross and end at the cross and make a rope or ladder to heaven. We pray the rosary with reverence and meditatively as we contemplate each mystery of the rosary. We reflect on the lives of Jesus and His Blessed Mother shared together. Two hearts, the most Sacred Heart of Jesus and The Immaculate heart of Mary beat as one. Mary was set apart in the entire human race for all time, chosen by The Father, chosen for The Son, chosen to be the bride of The Holy Spirit. Take the time and read The Apostolic Letter of Pope Saint John Paul II, on The Most Holy Rosary, "Rosarium Virginis Mariae". I invite all people to pray the rosary. You don't have to be Catholic to pray this great prayer.

The chaplet of Divine Mercy is to be prayed daily. I encourage you to read the diary of St. Faustina, the Apostle of Divine Mercy. It is a great meditative prayer about Redemptive suffering.

There are numerous other prayers. Pick one and take baby steps as faith is a gift, your response, and a life-long process.

Here is a time to pause and not be overwhelmed with all the prayers I mention or pray personally.

Your prayer life is personal, and you don't have to do what I do or as much. Start by making a commitment to one prayer. Consider going to daily mass, praying the rosary or praying other prayers you are comfortable with or have learned from your faith tradition, if not Catholic.

Focus and commit to one prayer daily and let the Holy Spirit lead you from there. You can make your prayer personal and in your own words. You may want to journal, which I recommend. I encourage you to read about "Lectio Divino", an ancient prayer form of the church which I also practice. It focuses on reading a scripture passage, praying on it, meditating on it, and finally contemplating it.

The next few paragraphs reveal my daily prayer routine.

In addition to the above prayers of the church, I pray and recite my own personal mission statement that I wrote several years ago: "To Glorify God in business and life, while helping others along the way".

I pray the 33 days to morning glory prayer, the St Patrick Prayer, The St Francis prayer, St. Michael

The Archangel defend us in battle prayer, the Anima Christi prayer, the angelic warfare confraternity prayers, the Beatitudes, the 10 Commandments, the fruits of The Holy Spirit, The Gifts of The Holy Spirit, the 7 deadly sins, the corporal works of mercy, the spiritual works of mercy, the 7 Dolors of Mary, and the following favorite Scripture passages:

"I have the strength for everything through him who empowers me" – Philippians 4:13. (This is the first bible quote I memorized and was given to me as a gift from my brother Kenny).

"Giving thanks always and for everything in the name of our Lord Jesus Christ to God the Father." - Ephesians 5:20

"Better to take refuge in the LORD / than to put one's trust in mortals." – Psalm 118:8

"My soul proclaims the greatness of the Lord; / my spirit rejoices in God my savior." – Luke 1:46-47

"For God so loved the world that he gave his only Son, so that everyone who believes in him might not perish but might have eternal life." – John 3:16

"But seek first the kingdom [of God], and his righteousness, and all these things will be given you besides." - Matthew 6:33

"We know that all things work for good for those who love God, who are called according to his purpose." – Romans 8:28

"Train a boy in the way he should go; / even when he is old, he will not swerve from it." – Proverbs 22:6

"As iron sharpens iron, / so man sharpens his fellow man." – Proverbs 27:17

[Then Jesus said, "**Father, forgive them**, they know not what they do."] – Luke 23:34 (emphasis added)

"Lord, do not hold this sin against them." – Acts 7:60

"What profit is there for one to gain the whole world and forfeit his life?" – Mark 8:36

"Before I formed you in the womb I knew you." – Jeremiah 1:5

"It is easier for a camel to pass through the eye of a needle than for one who is rich to enter the kingdom of God." – Matthew 19:24

"Jesus looked at them and said, 'For human beings this is impossible, but for God all things are possible.'" – Matthew 19:26

"This is the day the LORD has made; / let us rejoice in it and be glad." – Psalm 118:24

"My grace is sufficient for you, for power is made perfect in weakness." – 2 Corinthians 12:9

Jesus in me, loves you!

The Lord be with you! And with your spirit!

The Cross before me, the world behind me! (That prayer comes from my father).

Faith is not meant to be alone. It must be practiced and shared.

Those who say they have their own relationship with God, don't need to practice it with anyone, don't need a priest, and don't need to confess my sins to another person are deluding themselves. We need to have a personal relationship with God, but we need to be born again. We absolutely need to worship with a community of believers on a regular basis, and we also need to meet with a small faith based group regularly. This is how we learn and grow in our faith and sharpen each other.

Humility, Humility, Humility, helps us go deeper.

Humility comes from the Latin "humilis", which literally means low. In the biblical sense Jesus tells us:

"Blessed are the poor in Spirit..." (Matthew 5:3) and

"For the Son of Man did not come to be served but to serve..." (Mark 10:45).

Acting in humility does not mean we are a doormat. On the contrary, we act quietly and confidently. We are secure in God's love for us as His child, doing His work, serving Him in and through our fellow man. We put others before and ahead of us willingly and lovingly. We are truly happy for another when he or she succeeds.

The Church, in its infinite wisdom, given to us by Jesus the Christ Himself some 2000 years ago is a gift. Listen to IT! "...and to walk humbly with your God." – Micah 6:8

Chapter 17
Hey, what about me? I am married!

I hope and pray the principles and lessons given in this book can help married people as well. I hope you hold your spouse in the highest esteem of love called Agape love (putting the highest good of the other, a spouse in this case above your own good).

The key is Jesus in everything we do.

What is your mission? Write it down and recite it, pray it and act on it daily.

Love God with your entire will and being. Help others and be happy for them in their success, especially our spouses or ex-spouses.

Love conquers all and lifts us up to speak and act in encouraging others. Spouses, have deep respect for each other. Pray together, with, and for each other. Pray with and for your children, if you are blessed with children.

Live as Jesus taught us to live. Act as Jesus acted. Love as Jesus loved, with selfless sacrifice!

God bless and keep walking!

Part III

A Collection of Poems by
La Famiglia about our
family to help lift you up
and deepen your
relationship with God.

This is a collection of poems about my family members written by family members. This is my family of origin and heritage. My ancestors originate from Italy and surnames are DeFeo, Gentile, Pacetti and Cavarocchi.

On my father's side my Great Grandparents were Anthony and Rose DeFeo and Carmine and Catarina Gentile. All were born in Italy in The Campania province. My grandparents were Charles and Carmela "Millie" (Gentile) DeFeo. They were born in or brought to America at a very young age.

My father is Robert Charles DeFeo. He had one brother and one sister, Alexander Joseph and Roseann (McGraw) DeFeo. I had one sibling, my older brother Kenneth Charles DeFeo. All of my family members mentioned above have passed on from this life to the next.

On my mother's side my Great Grandparents were Giuliano and Elodia Pacetti and Gaetano and Bettina Cavarocchi. All were born in Italy in the provinces of La Marche and Abruzzi respectively. My grandparents were Adam and Rosalia "Rose" (Cavarocchi) Pacetti. They were also born in or brought to America at very young age. My mother is Elodia "Dee" (Pacetti) DeFeo and she has two siblings Julius "Jules" Pacetti and Nina (Pacetti) Robinson. All three are with us, and the rest mentioned above have passed on from this life to the next.

I am richly blessed to remain in contact with all members of the families I mentioned above. I remain in contact with them in a uniquely special and loving way. I am thankful and grateful for each of them in my life.

On the Gentile side we have bi-annual large family reunions. I am part of our family committee who makes these reunions happen. We call ourselves La Famiglia Gentile. My grandmom Millie was one of eleven children.

In the Gentile family, we also have a number of gifted writers and my inspiration for writing came from my Uncle and god-father, Alexander Joseph DeFeo, who penned a number of poems.

My grandpop, Adam Pacetti was a gifted and avid painter, and loved to read books.

My Father, I called him Pop, Robert Charles DeFeo, wrote many notes and had a way with words. He delivered many of the eulogies at family funerals. He was a great coach and life teacher.

This book contains poems and writings from members of the DeFeo and Gentile families.

Chapter 18
The Poems and Writings
of Alexander Joseph DeFeo

He was affectionately known as Uncle Alex. He was my uncle (My Dad's older brother) and also my godfather. He was born on January 20, 1926 and entered into Eternal Life on January 28, 1997.

We are the Marines

It dates back to Parris Island in the year of "43"
Our everlasting practice carried every Marine to sea
The Marines are a combat outfit who fight for
freedom's cause
We carry the word to the letter and live by Martial
Laws

We were first taught to use a rifle, a rifle not a gun
It is our utmost treasure, without it we are done
Our past is not forgotten; it lives on throughout the
years
We've suffered death and torture, and even shed
some tears

We were hardened at Parris Island and taught never
to retreat
But to make a perilous journey success and not
defeat
We've proven this our fact by Midway, Guam and
Wake
While in these Solomon jungles our lives are now at
stake.

We dig another foxhole, chop down another tree

We're always on the lookout, we're fighting
    constantly
We fight in small patrols, the jungle way you know
Our losses are quite great, our deaths are very slow

We're in these Solomon Jungles, and 5,000 miles
    from you
We miss your bedtime stories, and big bright eyes of
    blue
We're fighting for your freedom as well as for our
    own
We're tough and hardened "Girenes", but wish we
    were back home.

A Japanese patrol moves out; we attack them hand
    to hand
Our endurance is what counts, we're fighting man to
    man
Our Paris Island practice is now put into effect
Without that vigorous training we'd be a total wreck

At six the sun shines bright and high above the trees
There is the stars and stripes, she's waving in the
    breeze
Although we are outnumbered, Old Glory she still
    waves

Some proud Marines who fought for her, are resting
   in their graves
This very sight inspires us to keep her waving high
Another day begins, we are prepared to die
A prayer begins the day, and then we're off to war
We've whipped 10,000 Japanese and we'll whip
   10,000 more.

October 10, 1943

Dryland Sailor

The Navy brought me here to stay, upon the Norfolk
beach
Tied up beside the dock I lie, no ocean will I reach
Out in the bay the sun shines bright, the beauty of
the sea
And on my barge I sit and think that there's the place
for me.

In childhood days my memory dreamed, while
sitting on the cleat
That the future I would be a sailor of the fleet
And now at last my day has come, but still I have no
ship
This Norfolk beach must like me here; it tightens on
its grip.

Not far from me some ships pull in returning from
the seas
And loaded now they're off again, they're busier
than bees
Each deck is bordered with their crew, they blend
into the sky
And I a sailor on the beach can't look them in the
eye.
May 20, 1944

Charles DeFeo

Missionary Sister

It started out on Broad Street in 1935
When a little Catholic girl began her religious drive
At this Missionary convent her religious practice
    grew
While growing closer to her God, a goal now came
    in view.

In her little heart so pure, appeared a vision of a Nun
Which made her think that Nun was she, and now
    her work begun
And then one night out of the sky, a vision said to go
And bring here faith across the sea to those who did
    not know.

She parted for a convent in Upper New York State
For several years of practice to bring souls close to
    her mate
On a sunny day in August, she became a mission
    Nun
After thirteen years of prayer and work, her training
    was now done.

A few short days were spent at home with Dad and
    Mother dear

and then from LaGuardia field she'd part to an island
    far from here
To the Island of St. Croix she'd go, and waiting on
    the beach
Will be many of God's children for this Mission Nun
    to teach.

Her teachings by the Mission Mothers could now go
    in effect
She appreciates all their efforts in preparing for this
    trek
On this Island as years go by and souls come close
    to Jesus Christ
A Mission Nun has helped the cause because of her
    great sacrifice.

Although we will not see her, we'll pray for her each
    day
And our reward will be her prayers which will not
    come as pay
But as a lift toward heaven, where someday we will
    meet
And live in happy Paradise with God in his retreat.

May God Bless you & Guide You Always
TO: My Aunt, Sister Marie Carmine
    August 29, 1948

119

Our Immortal Mom

We are the children of your house, you helped put
    us on earth
Your life was full of sacrifice, we did not know its
    worth
Harbored within that gentle heart, were pain and
    sorrow great
When we were hurt, we came to you, you were our
    closest mate.

With outstretched arms you welcomed us, our
    Guardian next to God
But now the book of life has closed, you'll rest
    beneath the sod
When Heaven's gates are open and God will judge
    your worth
He'll tell his sacred helpers "Make room for a queen
    from earth".

For you there was no fanfare, no glory nor a throne
No trumpets loudly playing nor bugles ever blown
Unceasing days of hardship were all you ever knew
To make of us a family proud, as only you could do

And now that you will leave, within us you will live

For we still are your children, whom you've raised
from the crib
We'll try to make you proud of us, while in Heaven
you will rest
For we are blood from your own veins, blood of the
very best

When all the flowers wilt away, and generations
pass
These words of praise will still remain, until the very
last
In years to come when we pass on, to the world
where you now live
You'll start the house up once again, and raise us up
to Him.

June 21, 1952

The Rope to Eternity

God stretches it from heaven, to the earth far down
below,
This rope serves as a guiding way which shows us
where to go,
To climb up is not easy, a difficult feat to try,
Should we abide by the laws of God, we'll top it
when we die.

The way of life seems very hard when our faith is
not intact,
Therefore, we cannot reach the top, we'll fall down
on our back.
But if we're always faithful, then God can lift our
weight,
Making our effort easy, towards reaching the
heavenly gate.

In childhood days we're near the top, we stay there
all the time,
Occasionally we do fall down, but there's not much
to climb,
Should God decide to call us, during golden days of
youth,
Our life's climb will be easy; we'll always find out
the truth.

If we pass on from childhood, we grow up as adults,
The climb becomes much harder; we need strength
    for results.
Our daily life's temptations increase with every
    year,
But should we call on God for help, we'll always
    find him near.

Now as we pass the middle years, temptations will
    be less,
Cause inside us there grows some fear, we know
    soon we will rest.
The distance seems to narrow, the rope is not so
    high,
This feat, which we once thought was hard, is easy
    if we try.

As years go by, and we grow old, our life span soon
    will end,
We will grow mellower each day, like children once
    again.
Our strength is gone with passing years, no effort do
    we need,
To climb this rope, cause we're on top, it's worth it,
    yes indeed.

Should you be like the millions, who look up this
   rope and say,
How can I ever climb it, Heaven's farther every day?
No matter what age group you're in, or how you
   stand right now,
Keep faithful to your God above, and He will show
   you how.

Once you are inside Heaven, you'll reminisce and
   say,
The rope from here still stretches down, to show
   them all the way.
Someday they'll all be like me, they'll rest beneath
   the sod,
But only bodies will be there, their souls, will be
   with God.

August 7, 1953

Never Give Up

Keep your chin up always look up
God knows where you are each day
Though the days are dark and dreary
Never give up always pray

There will be a bright tomorrow
And you will smile once again
God will help to make you happy
He will be your lasting friend.

April 7, 1955

God's Little Flower

Created with God's gentle hand, a flower clean and
    pure
An angel from a distant land, her destiny is sure
A lily white she'll someday be, if she would only try
To dedicate her life to God, until the day she'll die.

He'll shower rays of sunlight, upon his Little Flower
And give her many graces, to help her by the hour
Now as the years go by, and she will find her place
God's Little Flower's happiness, will shine from her
    Angelic face.

Someday when she goes back, and visits St. Joe's
    home
She will inspire other girls; that they must never
    roam
She'll tell them all to listen, to that Mother Manuel
    taught
And then in Heaven they will find the happiness they
    sought.

January 2, 1956

I wrote "God's Little Flower" for a little girl I knew
who was put in a home for hooking school. She

126

came from a broken home and had two strikes against her. I thought a little inspiration may help her take the right road.

Charles DeFeo

Queen of Heaven

Blessed Mother, Queen of Heaven, guide me
through each day of life
I a humble sinner beg you, help me during time of
strife
When the devil sends temptation, counter act with
God's own grace
For it's God who made you Mother, of the sinful
human race.

January 2, 1956

I wrote Queen of Heaven to inspire me during time
of temptation. Even though I am not what I should
be I know the Queen of Heaven is always near to
help me.

My Mother

I argue with you daily
I often make you sad
But you're still the greatest Mother
That a little boy could have

I love you very dearly,
Even though I make you cry,
For you're my prize from heaven
And without you I would die.

March 16, 1956

My Mother's 50th birthday inspired me in writing this poem. Though there are not many words, they have deep meaning to me. She is my prize possession on earth. None can take her place.

Charles DeFeo

God's Test

If your heart is full of sadness, and your body full
of pain
If your pockets are all empty, and you suffer
mental strain
If you hate to see tomorrow, and you haven't got a
friend
It is only just a cycle, which will very shortly end.

If materially you're a pauper, and physically your
unsound
If you haven't got a home, and you're sleeping on
the ground
If it's you who's been selected, through these daily
trying tests
Then just face the world with laughter, it will pay
off when you rest.

If you lift your head up skyward, and a vision you
could see
If it gives you strength and courage, and assured
eternity
If his arms are both extended, and these gestures
make you cry

Then just pray you've been selected for His
   Household when you die.

April 10, 1956

A Sinner Returns Home

I drifted far away from God, to the lowly life of sin,
I left the Communion Rail behind, and the devil
 sprung within.
Like a cancerous growth he poisoned me, and I was
 all to blame,
And for ten long years I was no good, as I lived my
 life in shame.

Each day I traveled farther along, the wrong side of
 the track,
From all good teachings I had learned, I turned my
 sinful back.
The Communion Rail had drifted far, it was now out
 of sight,
And I who do belong to God, now left his guiding
 light.

These years for me were miserable, I was a lonely
 guy,
The people who had faith in me, I know I made them
 cry.
From the pits of sin, I saw no light, only darkness
 every day,
For causing God this sorrow, my debt I now must
 pay.

Dear Jesus, Mary and Saint Teresa, I'll thank them
    everyone,
For they have guided me back home, a new life I've
    begun.
I'll pray to all of them each day, and believe me God
    I'll try,
Before I ever sin again, I wish that I would die.

The Communion Rail's in sight now, I'll go there
    every day,
and pray dear God to keep me good, to live no other
    way.
With every days Communion, and God within my
    soul,
I found what I've been looking for, Heaven is now
    my goal.

October 17, 1956

The Millionaire
How Does He Stand With God?

Some man I know is a millionaire, at home they say
    he's good
A power in each state affair, a pillar in his
    neighborhood
He travels round the world each year, he walks on
    foreign sod
My friends, I ask one question, "How does he stand
    with God?"

Respected for his money, a genius in his field
His friends will tip their hats to him, at work he is a
    wheel
No project leaves the office, without his final nod
My friends, I ask one question, "How does he stand
    with God?"

Some people wish that they were he and buy their
    way with gold
They think their wealth will buy them health, and
    happiness untold
He owns a plane and fishing yacht, complete with
    every rod
My friends, I ask one question, "How does he stand
    with God?"

With all his many millions, there's something he
    can't buy
His entrance into Heaven when it's his time to die
To all of us who envy him, when he is 'neath the sod
We'll look and ask each other, "How did he stand
    with God?"

November 22, 1956

Charles DeFeo

The Crucifix

I kneel before the Crucifix, and sometimes I will cry
For it is I who put Him there, and also helped Him
    die
He gave his life for everyone, He showed us all the
    way
To everlasting happiness, if only we obey.

Each time I sin the wounds seem deep, the blood is
    glowing red
The nails must tear his flesh apart, the thorns must
    rip His head
And yet with gentle kindness, He always seems to
    say
My Son I will forgive your sins, return to me and
    stay.

And He will take me back with Him, and never will
    I part
For from the Cross I now have learned, I must not
    pierce His heart
The Crucifix shows sorrow, but in Heaven I will
    see
The happy face of Jesus for all eternity.

December 13, 1956

Our Immortal Pop

I remember Grand pop from the time I was a boy,
He always filled the ice box and filled our hearts
    with joy,
His home was always open to strangers as to kin,
He would always think of others even to the very end.

He was kind and quite soft hearted, although
    sometimes he was stern,
For this was his way of teaching and it really helped
    us learn.
Of the family that he started none disgraced him,
    none are bad,
For the discipline he ruled us, and today we all are
    glad.

He would work hard every day, that God gave him
    his life,
He was good to all his children, and especially to his
    wife
He had aches and pains and heartaches, still he
    trodded along life's way,
Pushing cars, selling flowers, sometimes farming all
    the day.
Though his work was not professional, it was honest
    as could be,

137

And with sweat, toil, and labor, he did raise his
    family,
Every member quite respectful from the discipline
    he stressed,
Ever striving, ever hopeful that we would turn out
    the best.

All his teachings and his training will live on
    throughout the years,
If we all set fine examples, and we never cause him
    tears,
His work on earth completed and his mark on
    everyone,
He has left us for a different world, and a new life
    has begun.

His record will go to Heaven, where he now will
    meet his mate,
She'll be waiting for her husband, and escort him
    thru God's gate.
Our earthly king will enter and he'll kiss her then
    he'll smile,
Let us hope we all will join them, even though it
    takes a while.

June 26, 1958

Parent

P - is for the PENANCE that I give you

A - means ALEX and I am your boy

R - is for the RIGHTEOUSNESS within you

E - means EVERY day you bring me joy

N - is for the NICE things you have taught me

T - is for the TEARS I cause each day

Put them all together they spell

PARENT

And you are the best in every way.

December 25, 1958

This was a Christmas present to my Mom and Pop in 1958. I got the idea from the song Mother. M is for the million things you gave me. O means only that you're growing old and so on.

My Family

Before the Altar of God at St. Rita's Church, my
    Mom and Pop were wed
The bands of marriage that bound them, would link
    them till both were dead
They took their vows to face this life, no matter how
    rough the way
No matter how great the hardships were, their love
    increased each day.

As years went by and we were born, Robert,
    Roseann and me
The hand of God has created life, and made us a
    family
We sometimes fight and argue, and make each other
    cry
But we still are the DeFeo's, and will be until we die.

Yes, we are human, and we do sin, we even make
    mistakes,
with all our faults and errors, we still have what it
    takes.
Some people may not think of us, as a model family
But in God's eyes I know we've tried, and he will
    map our destiny.

As years go by we may travel, each one a different
   way
But the brand that is DeFeo, is with each of us to stay
And proudly we will wear this brand, dear God I
   know we'll try
To be a model family, until the day we die.

My name is Alex, I have this say, my Family is the
   best
In a world of many millions, its distinguished from
   the rest.
My love runs deep for Mom and Pop, Roseann and
   Robert too.
Thank God you made them my Family, as only you
   could do.

When I will die and cannot speak, these words will
   speak for me
Of an average boy who tried his best, who really
   loved his Family
And God I hope in Heaven, the DeFeo's all will be
The Family of Dear Jesus, for all eternity.

January 7, 1962

In Loving memory of my sister Roseann. I wrote this poem in honor of my family. To me my family is the greatest family on earth. My Mother and Father did a great job with what little education and great hardships they had through life. This poem is also in memory of my sister who passed away April 14, 1961. As a sister and daughter she was everything you could ask for. As a Mother she was second to none. She could really bear the title of "Mother" proudly. I do not know what the final decision will be, but I feel my Father and Mother were blessed with a Daughter who is destined to become a Saint.

My Father

I would like to propose a toast to a man, who is religious, honest and kind. A man who is humble, modest and persevering. A type of man who when awards or "pats on the back" are to be given out, would not push himself to the front of the stage, but stay in the background. A man who never liked degrading or talking bad about anyone. A man who, even though I may of disagreed with at times, never once in all the years I knew him, gave me a wrong bit of advice. Some of you may think you know this man, but you know him for only minutes or hours or a few days. To really know a person, you must live with them for a long period of time. When you see someone for a short period of time they usually put their best foot forward. That is why I am sure I can say I know this man very well. You see I have been with this man 37 years and know him for at least 32 of those 37 years.

I do not think any Son is more proud than I am, to say the man I am writing about is my Father, Charles DeFeo.

"May he always be blessed by Almighty God."
February 6, 1963

Charles DeFeo

An Island Called Man

Each Man is an island, alone in the sea
When it's time to suffer, and face his destiny
As the storm hits the shore, causing damage and rain
A man may be called, to face intense pain.

He braces himself, for the days may be long
As the rolling seas howl, and the wind becomes
    strong
Though battered and beaten, and brought to his
    knees
This island called man, must not sink 'neath the seas.

When the storm passes over, and the sun it is bright
With God on the island, this man won his fight
The island is bright with the new morning sun
Its outlook is different, a new life begun.

This island called man, will thank God with me
That he did not sink beneath the rough sea
But someday he'll sink, and there'll be no more sod
His island is dust; his soul goes to God.

June 18, 1963

A Guy Named Joe

He's just a guy named Joe to you, but what a man is
he
The bravest man I ever met on land or on the sea
The courage that's within his heart, is too great to
explain
A man who's been through many tests, and suffered
every pain.

Whatever God has set for him, I'm sure he'll meet
the test
In all the world you travel, Gilroy ranks the best
When God calls him to Heaven, and Joe's soul will
be saved
He'll put him with a special group, the bravest of the
brave

June 18, 1963

The Nurse

An angel's smile a pleasant face,
No medicine can take her place
To me her work is never done
She seems to work from sun to sun
She does not stop nor will complain
Her gentle hands help relieve pain
She helps the sick from getting worse,
and proudly wears the title "Nurse".

She's in the room then out again,
She takes your pulse then dumps a pan
She brings the food and sometimes feeds,
She administers to all your needs
Though she is human and makes mistakes,
She still has everything it takes
Whatever words are in this verse,
I cannot praise enough the "Nurse".

Throughout her life this mark she'll bare,
and it will show most everywhere
An Angel who dear God did pick,
To help mankind and heal the sick
And when to Heaven she will go
I think dear God who runs the show

Will crown her then may read this verse
"Into Heaven Goes Every Nurse".

June 18, 1963

These 3 poems were written by a coward who fears death and pain.

John F. Kennedy, My President

A man of peace, a man of God, in Arlington rests
    'neath the sod
A bullet has cut short his life and made a widow of
    his wife
The nation mourns this man so great, and everyone
    will meditate
He'll always dwell within man's mind, for he was
    honest, good and kind.

A humble man who loved the poor, he fought for
    freedom on every shore
He wanted men to live as one, and put away their
    deadly gun
The world may someday reach his goal, and peace
    will enter mankind's soul
In this way all could live in peace, in a world where
    love would never cease.

His body's dust, his soul lives on, and we will see
    with every dawn
John F. Kennedy's immortal name, throughout the
    world will light the flame
His body rests in a hero's grave, from Heaven he'll
    see the world he saved

He gave his life that man may live, no greater gift
    can a human give.
November 27, 1963

On January 15, 1964, a thank you note for this poem
was sent from The White House's Ralph A. Dungan,
special assistant to the President on behalf of
Lyndon B. Johnson.

On January 23, 1964 another thank you note for this
poem was sent from The White House's Pierre
Salinger, Press Secretary to the President, Lyndon
B. Johnson.

South Philly

You may travel the world over, you may go from
   east to west
You may climb the highest mountain, still you
   haven't seen the best.

It lies between two rivers, South Street, it's normal
   end
To the Navy Yard on the Delaware, every stranger
   is your friend.

There are some who do not like it, though their
   choice is very bad
I was blessed with being born there, for this I'm very
   glad.

People move and some will leave it, yet it's part of
   them always
South Philly is their trademark, even to their dying
   days.

Yes, the section is South Philly, the best spot in the
   world
Where today's prominent man and woman, were its
   yesterday's boy and girl.

No matter where you travel, they can tell from where
   you came
For to be born in old South Philly, is my only claim
   to fame.

May 10, 1964

My Love for My Mother...

My love for my Mother is very great, even though I may have brought her hardship and tears. Sometimes I may not have been what she expected of me, for this I am sorry. I hope God forgives me for all injustices I may have committed towards her. My Mother had a very hard life on earth. When her time comes to leave this earth, I know God will take her up to Heaven with him.

February 12, 1968

Mother and Heaven both have six letters. My Mother (even though we had our differences) could bear the title of Mother well. Heaven is where I know she is now. Both Mother and Heaven belong alongside Carmela DeFeo's name, who even though she has passed on to Heaven will always be my Mother.

The Mountain of Life

The mountain of life stretches thru the clouds,
to the Heavens far up above
and it's climbed with blood, sweat, toil and tears,
but most of all with love.

It's not easy to get to the mountain peak,
where the beauty and peace await
And eternal happiness is yours,
once you're thru the Heavenly Gate.

You work and suffer, get old and sick,
and in time even loved ones die
And the setbacks are many as you slide down the
    hill,
but you pick yourself up and you try.

You think you're smart and know it all,
if you have your health, wealth and fame
The climb may seem easy and effortless,
but you haven't won the game.

You need compassion, humility and love,
as you await your judgment and fate
If it wasn't a struggle to reach the top,
at the Gate of Heaven, you'll wait.

153

If the mountain climb of life was rough,
and you reach the High Heavens above,
Then God will open the gate real wide,
and welcome you in with his love.

April 23, 1980

If this poem helps to brighten someone's sad life, and gives them courage to keep trying, then it will have served its purpose. Wherever I'll be, I'll be happy knowing in some small way to have helped a poor soul to see the light above the mountain top.

The River of Life

The river of life appears to be very wide
as you start your journey across
And the current is swift and seldom calm,
as your body begins to toss
With the guidance of God, you muster your
    strength,
as you swim to the far distant shore
As the waves splash your face, it's a difficult task,
but you call on your body for more

Disappointments and hardships are part of the
    swim,
as you go through your daily life
And you ache and pain, and you want to quit,
as ahead you see nothing but strife
If you lift your head up and look to the sky,
you'll see a friendly face
Who'll give you a push across the stream,
and help you win the race.

No goal comes easy to man on earth,
no river is easy to cross
With God at your side then nothing is hard,
God shows the river whose boss
Now that you've reached the far distant shore,

the beauty and peace make you sigh,
For you're now in Heaven, and happiness is yours.
You've reached the big sea in the sky.

April 27, 1980

My Dear Wife

I am broke and have no flowers,
still my Love is quite sincere
And of all my friends and Loved Ones,
You're the one that I hold dear
Through my suffering and my troubles,
you have proved to me my worth
And in spite of many setbacks,
You've made Heaven here on Earth.

You're a woman who can do,
anything that is expected.
And to anyone who knows you
You will always be respected.
Unselfishness is your trademark,
as we both go through this life.
You're my Queen, and you're my partner,
but you're most of all my Wife

Written from my heart on our 4th Anniversary,
October 1, 1981.

Love,
Alex

Charles DeFeo

Beyond Their God Given Talents
– The Brothers DeFeo

They both played football, and played it quite well
From grade school through College, these two did
  excel.

They gave away height, they gave away weight
Intensity and courage, is what made them both great.

They captained their teams, wherever they played
They're natural born leaders, and good at their trade.

Brother Ken made his mark in the South USA
Where he's loved and respected even unto this day.

Young Charles who is smaller plays for a small
  school,
As a 5'7" nose guard appears 7 feet tall.

At Bonner, O'Hara, Ursinus and State
is where they developed and molded their fate.

And someday when God calls each one he'll tell
On the Gridiron you both served your time in Hell.

Written by Uncle Alex DeFeo on November 1, 1984

The Outpost

It's three miles from 69th Street, but a hundred
    miles away
It's a family bar with men, who meet there every
    day.
Joe O'Donnell is the owner, a man who's fair and
    kind
And the Manager is Bob DeFeo, the best you'll
    ever find.

It's a sports bar featuring football, mainly O'Hara
    and Bonner High.
These O'Donnell men are loyal, and will be until
    they die.
The fans of these two High Schools, meet each
    Friday night at seven
And to drink and root at the Outpost is a ticket up
    to Heaven.

October 12, 1987

Jimmy Coz and Gigi "O"

Jimmy Coz and Gigi "O"
are friends both tried and true
They're loyal guys - the best there are,
as friends they stand by you.

Both classy men who tell the truth
and speak an honest mind
They're street smart guys who have big hearts -
both men are good and kind.

They hold their own in football,
each root for local teams.
They help the younger players
fulfill their college dreams.

They have a zest for life,
and both believe in God.
To Football Heaven their souls will go
when their bodies are neath the sod.

Written in honor of Gigi O'Neill's 50th Birthday
and Jimmy Costello's 20th year in bringing winning
championships to Cardinal O'Hara football.

October 15, 1988

Dear Theresa

You are my life, you are my wife,
You make my life complete,

You work a job, you work at home,
You're always very sweet.

I feel so blessed to have you,
A lucky man am I.

I love you now and always will,
Until the day I die.

December 24, 1994

Charles DeFeo

Dear Theresa,

To the best of my ability I try to compensate you for making a beautiful married life for me. Though you can never really be compensated in material things, there is an abundance of love behind anything I do for you. I can best describe my feelings with these words.

I loved you from the first time that I met you,
I love you 'cause you help to make my life

I love you for a hundred thousand reasons,
But most of all I love you as my wife.

You really help to make the holidays bright. I appreciate all the work you do and all the money you spend on everyone. You are truly a generous woman who gives of her time and money.

Love,
Alex

December 25, 1996

The piece above was the last time my beloved Uncle Alex would write. He passed from this life into the next a month after he wrote this. He was born into this life on January 20, 1926 and he was born into eternal life on January 28, 1997. He now rests with his God and my God. He taught me much about faith in God and practical things in life and inspired me to write. He stood only 5'6" and had a heart of Gold. To me, he was a giant among men. He was always there for me and my family. His family.

Uncle Alex, I miss you dearly, but I will never forget you and you live on inside of me. Thank you for everything you did for me and for the family, our family. You made me laugh often and as you would like to say. You warmed my heart and many others with your humor and philosophy and caring attitude. You taught me to check and re-check and I do. You would say God bless you many times to me and others. I do too, because of you. So, I will close by saying, may God bless you, my Uncle and godfather, forever and may he shed His perpetual light upon you for all eternity.

Chapter 19
The Poems of Patti Borghesi

Patty is my cousin and my father's first cousin on my grand mom Carmela Gentile DeFeo's side. Amadeo Gentile was Patti's father. Amadeo was my grandmom Carmela's brother.

Charles DeFeo

A Poem for Alex

Who will write the poem for Alex?
I wonder who it will be
If I were but more talented,
I wish it could be me.

I'd tell of a dear cousin
So quiet and astute;
Of a picture I hold fondly
Of Alex in his sailor suit

I'd say how badly I felt for him
When his dear sister passed away;
A sadness that remained with him
Until his dying day.

Each time a happy or sad occasion took place
He'd muster up his feelings with style and grace;
And put upon paper with eloquence and speed
A history of our family for all of us to read.

There's a party in heaven
Of this I am sure
With my dad, his Uncle Amadeo
Welcoming him at the door.

Who will write the poem for Alex;
Tell of his gentleness and love?
Who will write the poem for Alex?
The Lord has written it from above.

Love,
Patti, His Cousin
Amadeo was her Dad
January 29, 1997

A Poem for My Mother Emma Gentile
who passed from this life to the next
on January 16, 2003.

I have written these lines for many another
How do you write on the death of your Mother?
You were up in age with a very bad heart;
But the unexpected death is tearing me apart.

We had made plans of what we'd do next week;
Now your final hours are the answers I seek.

We talked several times the day before;
If I'd known it would be our last, I'd have talked
    more and more.
I would have stayed on the phone forever talking of
    the past;
And how the years flew by ever so fast.

You held my hand when I was small on our many
    trips to CHOP;
I held yours in the end to try and make the suffering
    stop.

You gave so much in the best you knew how;
The soups, pizzelles, pasta; Who will stuff the
    calamari now?

You were tough, but with a soft inside;
That all your words and actions could never truly
hide.

You'd worry and fret, especially in the snow;
"Did everyone get home yet?" you wanted to know.

You loved all the babies as each one came;
So proud of them all - your claim to fame.

They say the apple doesn't fall far from the tree;
So I hope part of you still lives in me.

You've gone away, on a journey to Heaven you
roam;
Give me a ring, Mom, to let me know you're safely
home.

Patricia

Chapter 20
A Poem by Robert Charles DeFeo

My father, I called him Pop.

My Father, Robert Charles DeFeo, was a blue collar hard working union guy. That is the best way I can describe him. He also had great compassion for others and Passion for His God. He played and coached football and loved the game. He played football for St. Laurence grade school in Upper Darby, PA. He went on to play at West Catholic High School, and then for Temple University for one season. He left school after his freshman year to go to work. It was very important to him that my brother Kenny and I graduated college as he did not. We both honored him and graduated from college and he was so proud of us for that accomplishment.

He started coaching youth football at Westbrook Park boys club. He went on to become defensive coordinator at Monsignor Bonner High School where he coached from 1972-1976.

When he was head coach at Westbrook Park, they won back to back championships with the 95lb and 115lb teams. He wrote a poem on a napkin on the bus ride home from Annapolis, MD after his team won the Championship game in the fall of 1969. He was so proud of the boys. He wrote this poem in his own words to the music of "We Love You Conrad" from the musical "Bye Bye Birdie".

"We Love You Westbrook, Oh Yes We Do
We Don't Love Anyone As Much As You
When You're Not With Us We're Blue
Oh Westbrook We Love You"

There was a big pep rally and bonfire after this win honoring the team and it seemed like the entire town of Westbrook came out to celebrate with us.

I was 5 years old at the time, and my brother Kenny played on this team. My Mom Elodia was the cheerleaders coach. I will never forget it and so proud to be a DeFeo and part of Westbrook Park.

Many who played football for my Pop at Westbrook Park and Bonner High continue to say to me how much my father meant to them as a coach, teacher, mentor and father figure not just in football but in life. I am honored, humbled and proud to call him my Pop. It warms my heart very much to hear these kind words about him. He treated me and everyone he met with kindness. He was firm but fair, and he always told me, "It's nice to be important but more important to be nice". He had so many other great sayings and wrote notes often.

Love and miss you Pop. Thanks for being an angel on my shoulder now.

Chapter 21
A Poem by my Cousin Richard DelViscio about my Brother Kenneth Charles DeFeo, on Kenny's passing from this life to the next on December 28, 1997.

Richard wrote this poem in honor of Kenny's memorial service we celebrated memorializing Kenny's life on February 16, 1998 in Delaware County, PA where he grew up. Kenny's funeral service was on December 31, 1997 in Gallatin, TN where he lived. Many people that knew Kenny when he was younger and were unable to travel a great distance to pay respects at his funeral.

This poem was written by Richard, and he sent it to my parents and Kenny's parents (Robert and Elodia DeFeo) on February 16, 1998 in honor of Kenny's memorial service.

Uncle Tony Gentile (who Richard mentions in his dream below), was my great uncle and my grand mom Carmela Gentile's younger brother. He was a great athlete, and a tremendous swimmer. He played in the national handball championship held in Chicago in 1948. He also coached. My Uncle Alex loved him dearly, as he loved his entire family. He was very proud of his Uncle Tony's athletic accomplishments. My Uncle Alex used to drive many family members around. I will never forget that my Uncle Alex brought Uncle Tony to see both my brother Kenny and I play football when we were younger. Specifically, my Uncle Alex loved historic Franklin Field, home of The Penn Quakers football team. Franklin Field is where my brother Kenny played for Villanova in a game against Penn. My Uncle Alex brought Uncle Tony to that game. A few years later, and a short time before Uncle Tony passed, he brought him once again to Franklin Field to watch me play football for Ursinus College in a scrimmage game against Penn's JV football team. The image of my great Uncle Tony and my Uncle Alex sitting in the stands that day watching me play, still are a fixture in my mind.

Richard is the son of Richard DelViscio and Kathleen (Gentile) DelViscio. Richard is my Pop's first cousin. Kathleen is sisters with Patti (Gentile) Borghesi. They are the children of Amadeo Gentile, my grandmom, Carmela Gentile DeFeo's brother.

Richard's sister Carol (Amadeo family) is on the La Famiglia Gentile family reunion team along with me and 5 others. Jay Evans (Family of Marco), Tom

Frank (Family of Vera), Jim Curcio (Family of Tony), Andrea Parmer (Family of Rocco), EJ (Family of Art) and Charles DeFeo (Family of Carmela).

John (Uncle John) never married and had no children.

Anna was our missionary sister.

I Had a Dream the Other Night

I had a dream the other night that I wanted to share with you. I'll never understand why we dream what we do, I suspect Kenny's sudden passing has served to remind me of my own mortality and this was on my mind. Anyway, while I do not recall all the details of my dream, I do remember standing outside the gates of heaven. As I looked in, I saw Kenneth there with a man, the man's back was towards me so I could not see who it was. He was talking with Kenneth and had an arm around his shoulder. After a while, they started to walk away. As they did the man turned and I could see who it was...Uncle Tony Gentile. He nodded and smiled as if to say everything will be alright...then they both headed off together. I guess the Lord has a special place for all his athletes and Uncle Tony was taking Kenneth there.

Kenneth was a man of kindness and humility who cared deeply for others. His athletic prowess came from his incredible self-discipline and willingness to sacrifice. His friendly smile and genuine good-nature will be missed by all who came to know and love him.

As loving parents, you gave him to us and you should take pride in the son, the brother, the father, the friend... and the man, Kenneth came to be. I look at my own sons and pray they will grow into the men your two boys became...men of character and principle. It is readily evident they are men who understand that our destiny is greater than this earthly existence and consequently strive each day to make a better life for others.

I recall my year teaching at Monsignor Bonner while in the seminary. As I walked the halls, I was not known as Rich, the Augustinian seminarian, but rather, "Rich...Kenny DeFeo's cousin"! The faculty and coaches there who knew him all spoke so highly of Kenneth. The names of "DeFeo" and "Cappelletti" were used quite often when discussions of outstanding football players...and outstanding young men took place. I was proud to be his cousin.

I'll never forget when my Glenolden baseball team played Kenny's Westbrook Park team and Kenny and I each had a couple hits for our respective teams. I would come up to bat to see Kenny's smiling face behind his catcher's mask and I patted him on the back as he stood next to me on 3rd base after he slugged a triple. I guess blood is thicker than water. After the game as the two teams went their separate ways, Kenny and I left the field together and went to your house for a post-game pizza.

It is at times like these that I wished we all lived closer together to be with our family. And while we cannot see each other, rest assured of my thoughts and prayers for both of you. I wish I had cousin Alex's gift for prose and could put into poetic form more thoughts and reflections about Kenny. My feeble attempt yields only the following...

...For his loving parents, oh how incomplete their dream,
may they find solace in the Lord, for Kenneth now stars for His team.

He dons the earthly pads no more,
all strife and worries gone for sure,
For now, he lives at peace with the chosen few,
the example of his life leaving each of us so much
more to do."

With Loving Sympathy, I pray that The Lord will
bless you both.

Love,
Cousin Richard DelViscio
February 16, 1998

Chapter 22
The Poems of Carmine Gentile

He is my cousin and my Pop's first cousin and son of who we called Uncle Rocco. Uncle Rocco was the youngest of the eleven Gentile children. He was born to my Great Grandparents Catarina and Carmine Gentile. He was my grand mom Carmela Gentile DeFeo's baby brother.

Uncle John was Rocco's brother and my grand mom Carmela's younger brother. He never married. He was so good and kind to all of his nephews, nieces and great nephews and nieces.

The eleven Gentile children born to my Great Grandparents Carmine and Catarina Gentile were named (not in chronological order): Marco, Amadeo, Art, Tony, John, Rocco, Carmela (DeFeo), Anna (who became a missionary nun in The Catholic Church), Vera (Testa), Dominic and Giorgio. Dominic and Giorgio both of whom passed from this life to the next as infants.

This side of the family we call La Famiglia, and I am one of seven on this family committee. We have ongoing family reunions with many generations of family in attendance. It is always a special time when we gather together and celebrate our family history, the gift of family and life.

Tribute to "Father John"

He was a man of strong will
His love of God was his foundation
No Matter how different, he accepted all
He kept alive our family tradition

Himself was his gift to us all
For God's way was his belief
Family Historian he kept us fulfilled
Loving all he met in his walk of life

Proud of his heritage, such a man was he
To no one he shows any scorn
For this his legacy will not sleep
His love and generosity are well known

At his death bed's side, we all turned
To say Thank YOU for all the years
A respect indeed he earned
A man to all who was so dear

So we gather under the tree united
To ease a great sorrow is our reason
With God's family he is reunited
Uncle John, "A Man of all Season"

183

In Ending, I Thank God for the chance
To have lived with such a man
No matter where one's life branches
Uncle John will always do what he can

In Memory of Uncle John – died July 14, 1982

A Belated Good-Bye

In the still of the night you went to sleep
For your job here on earth is done
My eyes tear, my heart weeps
For God has called you home

Please come back, I have to talk
The time cannot be right
I need your help to take life's walk
The candle flickers, gone is the light

You were always there with open arms
Love pouring from your heart
Strength, protecting me from harm
Pride, even at times when you hurt

Your dreams was life itself
Respect and Tradition is what you taught
Faith and Hope were your beliefs
Love and Family were all you sought

Your Sister's words should be our drive
She says, "We do not fear death"
But the incompleteness of our lives
I now know, it is the truth

Charles DeFeo

You live with your family once again
Together in heaven, now your home
Everlasting happiness with no pain
To open God's doors when we come

To see you once more I pray
For I lost the chance to tell you
The words I always wanted to say
Pop, "I Love You"

Goodbye for now.

You're Son.
Carmine Gentile
December 25, 1985

Three Simple Words

Cloudless skies with stars in the night
Silence untouched by rains fall
Beauty, that is best of dark and light
Becomes part of love's call

She is beauty, part of love's call
She is help, always on the move
Indeed, she is best of all
Yet to me she gives her treasure of love

Her hair is soft and brown, yet light
Her smile is the heart of happiness
Her eyes are kind and bright
All this she gives to me

She has lips as soft as snow
A kiss which says I love you
She has hands of affection
With arms of attachment

They say romance is just a game
Yet to me her love is true
She is quiet with no fame
All this I know is true

187

Charles DeFeo

Desiring the best of all
In joy, happiness and love
She stops at me for fulfillment
I hope I'm worthy of such a girl

She is so beautiful to me
Yet I find it hard to express my love
Three Simple Words she wants to hear
So to my Sweetheart "I love you"

Carmine Gentile

Chapter 23
The Poems of Charles Adam DeFeo

Mom and Dad,

The other night I believe I was divinely inspired! I wrote all these poems in about 30 minutes. I do not know what happened to me. Everything just flowed out of me onto paper for the people who are dearest to me.

Love Charles
May 5, 1998

Our Immortal Ken

There was no one finer than the man we called Ken
He left us a legacy of what it takes to be a perfect ten

The world is divided into givers and takers,
Ken was truly a giver

His climb was steep, his love ran deep
And flowed like and endless river

He brought happiness and joy
Even when he was a little boy

By his patience, love and kindness he showed us all
how to be
He would bring out the best in all of us, especially
you and me

He feared God but no one else - he was the toughest
you would ever meet
His passion, intensity, courage and strength surely
could not be beat

Yes, he was a Godly man, both humble and meek
If you met him, it is the Lord you would seek

Now he is home with God
His body raised above the sod

His spirit is a part of me
I must be strong I cannot flee

When I feel sad and want to cry
I will look up to Heaven but will not ask why

We must love each other as he would want us to
And when we are called home he will be there to
   greet me and you!

For my beloved brother Ken

I wrote this poem for my mother and father as
Mother's Day and Father's Day approaches, their
first without their firstborn son Ken on earth. Mom,
I have been thinking about the words of the prophet
Simeon in the gospel of Luke. When Mary and
Joseph brought the baby Jesus to the Temple
according to the custom of the Law, Simeon blessed
them and said to Mary: "A sword will pierce through
your own soul also."

Mom, I know how your heart is broken and there is nothing I can do to repair it. For Ken and I, you are our mother and you gave us life. Ken and I both know there is no other like you. You are special. Please pray for Mary's intercession, our Blessed Mother, who I know you love and are devoted to, for May is her month. I know she is the one who understands and can help heal your broken heart. She went through what you went through.

Thanks to you and Pop, I have been praying the rosary daily in my car each morning on my way to work. I have come to realize that the best and surest and quickest way to The Sacred of Heart of Jesus is through the Immaculate Heart of His Mother and Our Blessed Mother. They are two flesh Hearts that beat as one! Remember you and Pop sent me the rosary beads and the booklet on how to say it. Thanks for doing that.

Happy Mother's Day we love you! Your loving sons Kenneth and Charles.

May 4, 1998

My Brother

There is a picture of Ken and me that I keep up on my wall for all to see.

I was three, he was seven and his love for me reached up to Heaven!

May 4, 1998

Charles DeFeo

My Mother's Love

My mother's love for me is real,
So genuine no one can conceal;

She praises everything I ever do,
A number one fan for me and you.

She devoted herself to three men;
Robert, Kenneth and Charles, 1,2,3… not ten.

Where would we be without Mom,
Our Greatest Cheerleader with hand on pom-pom.

Yes, her love is deep and so real,
Our Queen on earth, she makes us feel…
ALIVE!

May 4, 1998

My Pop

He is my dad, I call him Pop,
He taught me everything, mostly how to stay on top.

Hard work was his game
Even if there came no fame.

He loved his family more than anything,
It was such a beautiful sight; it could make you sing.

We walk, we talk, we laugh, we cry
But most of all we pray on high.

Yes, he is my dad, I call him Pop
he gave me backbone...I will never flop.

May 4, 1998

Charles DeFeo

Sue

Her name is Sue
It rhymes with You

With her around
I'm never blue.

She is my lover, best friend and wife
But most of all she is my life.

May 4, 1998

Alex & Julia

Alex and Julia are their names,
They are little children and like to play games.

They are a sight to see,
so beautiful, innocent and loving I wish we all could
be.

One is three and one is five,
their happiness and joy keeps us all alive.

We love them so, it is plain to see
because they make us feel so free.

They've changed our lives,
They've touched our hearts

And both of them are so smart
But most of all, I hope and pray that our souls will
never part!

May 4, 1998

Charles DeFeo

My Friend

I have a friend, his name is Dave
He is always there for the save

If I am in trouble
he will not hesitate; For he is there on the double

If you have one friend in life like this, you need no
    other
For he will sticketh closer than a brother.

May 5, 1998

Sales

People will say to me sales is too rough,
This may be true but you must be tough enough.

When you love what you do, it is very easy,
With the Holy Spirit dwelling in your heart you
    will never become queasy.

Faith, determination, hope and perseverance
Will lead you to a successful clearance.

God's call is for you to be the best you can be in
    whatever you do…
So don't let Him down, be true to Jesus and you!

June 9, 1998

Charles DeFeo

My Christmas Prayer

Heavenly Father, what is Christmas all about?
Indeed, You sent your only Son to save us I have no
doubt.

You have showed us the way to eternal life; If we
just search and listen
Our hearts will truly shine and glisten.

Why is there so much suffering in the world we live
in?
Please help me to be strong and never give in.

Prayer is my strength and Your only weakness
Your Son Jesus taught us how to love with humility
and meekness.

Christmas day two thousand years ago is when it all
began
When the trumpets sounded and the Heavenly
Angels sang.

Our Mother Mary, Saint Joseph and all the
shepherds were there
Even though they were treated so unfair.

They put Him in a manger for the world to see
Our little baby Jesus would grow up to save you and
me.

How lucky we are God loves us so much…

Jesus, no greater love...no greater gift!!!

December 10, 1998

My Mom and Dad - 40 Years of Marriage

Happy Anniversary to two of the best...
They are my parents and their love has certainly
  been put to the test...

40 years of loving, caring and sharing is their
  motto...
Often you will find them praying in the Grotto...

What can I say, I am so proud...
I can climb the tallest mountain and shout my love
  for them aloud...

There have been ups and there have been downs...
But their passion for life makes them never frown...

They have had their share of adversity and
  heartache...
But they have put their lives in God's hands and in
  HIS trust they partake...

Whatever life brings I hope they always roll a lucky
  seven...
But this I know, they will be together forever in
  heaven!
March 20, 1999

The Bible

I love this book; it is such a part of me
It is the written Word of God; how can that be?

He uses man to carry out His will, be it ink on paper
Spoken words, deeds, actions or some other caper.

Prophets, teachers, elders, priests, kings and leaders
Have shown us what it takes to be called God's
    people
On the pages of this book.

But there is only one Master, His name is Jesus
Some Apostles and Gospel writers were Paul, Peter,
    Matthew, Mark, Luke, John and James
Who left us His Legacy by the power of The Holy
    Spirit.

Yes, God the Father, Son and Holy Spirit make up
    the Divine Trinity
I love this Book, it's called the Bible and it will live
    on for all Eternity!

November 30, 1999

The Blessing of Two More Children
Angela and Rosalie

Ang and Rosie, Rosie and Ang, these two came to
    us later
but brought so much joy!

Once we had Ang we knew we had to have
    Rosie…
Wild hair everywhere
Screams of laughter
Bundles of Joy!

They go together like PB&J
Duo Dances, snapchat and Insty
YouTube videos that make our hearts sing

Photography, Sports, Recitals and more
Creatively weaving their own path in life as we go
    for the score
And making us feel like teenagers again!

February 5, 2016

Another Set of DeFeo Kids We Love

DeFeo Kids south, the youngest a boy
We call him Guy, he came to us abnormally,
I mean to Sue and I

Moved North, fit right in
He sure gave us a win

His sisters Becca and Jenn still live in the South
USA
All grown up with their own families in tow

Life goes on - Death, Marriage and Birth -
The Family ever expands

Jacob, Melanie, Haleigh and Katy
Jordan, Chason and Layla Rose

Who's next, Can't wait!
DeFeo's in the North and DeFeo's in the South
This Family is truly a great Blessing to me and I
will always proudly scream that from my
Mouth!

February 5, 2016

Who are My Brothers and Sisters?

We call ourselves The Men of Faith
These men meet every week in brotherly love
Praising God in the form of The Dove

I have sisters in faith too
Who keep me true
So many friends to be thankful for
Old and New

Many brothers and sisters
Charismatics, Dominican's and others too
both wholesome and broken just trying to renew

But we are all in it together
Striving to be our best
For Our God, who sometimes puts us to the test.

We all make up the body of Christ
helping each other
Laughing, Living and sometimes crying

I am thankful for all my "brothers" and "sisters"
on this road called Life
I hope and pray I can help all attain Holiness as
    God would want us to

Without sad faces and strife

May we lift each other up in faith as brothers and
    sisters should do
and encourage all those we meet to strive to do the
    will of the Father as Jesus taught us to

Let's begin again Anew!!!

February 29, 2016

Charles DeFeo

La Famiglia Forever

DeFeo's, Gentile's, Pacetti's and Cavarocchi's
That's the brand I came from

La Famiglia keeps blending with each generation
In-Laws and newcomers ever on the march
Keeps me on my toes
I will never become starch!

All amazing people and a blessing in my life
Scattered East, West, North and South
I look forward to the reunions to come in the future
One step, one inning, one day at a time

Keep moving forward with joyful hope
Living, Loving, Laughing with all!

Proud of and thankful for this brand forever!!!

Epilogue

I am thankful to God for the gift of writing. It is such an honor and pleasure to write for you.

It is such a pleasure to share my family, friends and my faith with you, and my poems and the poems and writings of my dear loved ones.

This is such a labor of love for me, and it's all a gift and blessing from God.

He is my Rock and my Refuge. He has redeemed me and saved me.

I love my God. I love my family. I love my friends. I love all people. I am His child and Jesus is my Lord and King, my everything!!!

Through happiness, sadness, heartache and adversity I walk on in faith in God. He first showed me the way, and he uses others to help me starting with my family, whose shoulders I stand on. I stand on the shoulders of my Parents, Grandparents, Great Grandparents, Aunts, Uncles, Cousins and Friends along the way.

Earth is not my final destination. It's an awesome place and gift from God to me and you but I look to and hope for something much greater. Perfection in the abundant Life to come. In the meantime, I will strive to make this life as close to Heaven as possible by always striving to be the best version of myself every minute of the day regardless of who I am with or what I am doing.

I will continue to pray often and use words when necessary, always lifting up and never putting down.

I hope and pray you agree, and will join me to live an abundantly joyful life in Christ by walking by faith to live!

I have kept a journal since 1986 and I encourage you to keep a Journal as well. It is cathartic and life changing. It keeps you in a positive frame of mind. Write your heart's desire as often as you can, or as often as you like.

Follow your dreams and dream big. God wants you to do this.

Stay close to The Lord; His mercy endures forever.

St Paul tells us in his writings to persevere to the end. My mom and Pop told me that too. I listened to and learned from my parents. Their mantra was to put your heart and soul into anything and everything you do. Give it your all.

Jesus told us something similar when he summed up all the commandments and laws into two:

Love the Lord your God with all your heart, all your strength, all your mind, all your soul.

and

Love your neighbor as yourself.

That is all I try to do each and every day.

Keep on Walking by Faith to Live Forever!!!

God Bless!!!

Yours in Christ,
Mr. Charles A. DeFeo, O.P.

Armor of God – Battle against Evil
Ephesians 6:10-17

"Finally, draw your strength from the Lord and from his mighty power. Put on the armor of God so that you may be able to stand firm against the tactics of the devil. For our struggle is not with flesh and blood but with the principalities, with the powers, with the world rulers of this present darkness, with the evil spirits in the heavens. Therefore, put on the armor of God, that you may be able to resist on the evil day and, having done everything, to hold your ground. So stand fast with your loins girded in truth, clothed with righteousness as a breastplate, and your feet shod in readiness for the gospel of peace. In all circumstances, hold faith as a shield, to quench all (the) flaming arrows of the evil one. And take the helmet of salvation and the sword of the Spirit, which is the word of God".